THE MIRROR PRINCIPLE

Who do you
see when you look
in the mirror?

LAWRENCE P. LUBY

Copyright © 2008 by Lawrence P. Luby

All rights reserved. Except as permitted under the U.S. Copyright Act of 1976, no part of this publication may be reproduced, distributed, or transmitted in any form or by any means, or stored in a database or retrieval system, without the prior written permission of the publisher.

HIS Publishing Group
4310 Wiley Post Rd., Suite 201D
Addison, TX 75001
info@hispub.com

All scripture quoted in this book is from the New King James Version. Copyright © 1982 by Thomas Nelson, Inc. unless specified otherwise. Used by permission. All rights reserved.

Scripture quotations marked (NIV®) are taken from the Holy Bible, New International Version®, NIV® Copyright © 1973, 1978, 1984, 2011 by Biblica, Inc.® Used by permission. All rights reserved worldwide.

ISBN-13: 978-0-9973430-6-9   paperback
          978-0-9836367-6-2   hardcover

The Mirror Principle - Whom do you see when you look in the mirror? Summary: "Our life experiences form the basis by which we provided counsel and direction to others making us stronger along the way." —Provided by the publisher.
1. Self-Help / Business 2. Spiritual life 3. Inspirational

Printed in the United States of America

10 9 8 7 6 5 4 3

Division of Human Improvement Specialists, llc.

www.hispubg.com | info@hispubg.com

CONTENTS

INTRODUCTION MIRROR PRINCIPLE DEFINED	5
CHAPTER I MIRROR: POSITIVE REFLECTION	11
CHAPTER II EXPERIENCE: GUIDANCE	23
CHAPTER III INTERACTION: ACCOUNTABILITY & TRUST	35
CHAPTER IV REINFORCE: STRENGTH & COVERING	53
CHAPTER V TRANSFORMATION: POWER & PROPULSION	67
CHAPTER VI TRINITARIAN STRUCTURE: DESTINIES ALTERED	79
CLOSE ETERNAL LIFE	83
ABOUT THE AUTHOR	95
OTHER BOOKS BY THE AUTHOR	107

INTRODUCTION

Our current spiritual state expressed by our reflection in the mirror and our reflection to those around us.
—*Mirror Principle*

What if our life experiences formed the basis by which we provided counsel and direction to others? Additionally, what would happen if as we interacted and held each another accountable, our counsel and direction mirrored back, reinforcing and strengthening what we had already learned? Could it be that transformation would take place and lead us toward our eternal *purpose*? What if that which is stated in second Corinthians 3:18 is an indication of God's intended design for each of us?

> "But we all, with unveiled face, beholding as in a mirror the glory of the Lord, are being transformed into the same image from glory to glory, just as by the Spirit of the Lord"

Think of athletes preparing to compete in a contest. They will usually rise to the level to which they have pushed themselves previously and possibly beyond, depending on their ability and internal fortitude. However, when someone comes alongside, coaching, encouraging, and driving them, they are more likely to achieve greatness.

One would hope that the coach is qualified, having already traveled the path and knowing what it takes to reach the goal.

The same is true in business. Every great company has an excellent training program. The leaders of those companies understand the only way they will become great as a company is if their people become great.

There are many key ingredients in training people. The following are three of the most important:

- Providing and imparting knowledge
- Holding people accountable to that knowledge
- Rating performance

There are many benefits derived, but the following two are the most important:

- Existing leaders and the people they are mentoring become stronger.
- Transformation takes place.

Please note: I will be using the terms training, mentoring and discipleship interchangeably.

Introduction

The goal should be to create a culture of integrity, an adherence to a defined moral and ethical code so that people mirror biblical character; thus, building an interactive environment in order for them to pass on knowledge that will propel those who come behind them to go further and accomplish more, strengthening them all the while. The result becomes positive, ongoing transformation for years to come.

God accomplishes transformation by utilizing people through the process called discipleship. He calls his people to guide one another and to hold each other accountable to His Word. When the Lord calls people to steward other people through this type of relationship, He wants them to have an understanding of the following:

- God has approved them because of the reflection of Christ in their daily walk.
- They have specific experiential knowledge that God will use to mirror into another person's life.
- God intends for them to steward others through the process of discipleship, holding them accountable along their spiritual journeys.
- God uses their counsel to mirror, thereby reinforcing what they have learned and spiritually strengthens their relationship with Him.
- Both parties experience transformation by His mighty power and their eternal destinies are altered.

Therefore, discipleship at a core level is all about mirroring Christ. We share biblical truths allowing His counsel to penetrate our hearts and mirror bi-directionally, propelling each of us deeper in our walk with the Lord. It is a method of accountability modeled by Jesus' walk while here on earth and through His Word as provided in the bible.

> ¹Disciple—from the verb *manthano*, "to learn." Defined as a learner, one who follows both the teaching and the teacher. One who accepts and assists in spreading the doctrines of another as (a) one of the twelve in the inner circle of Christ's followers according to the Gospel accounts, (b) a convinced adherent of a school or individual.

> ²Accountability—the quality or state of being accountable; especially an obligation or willingness to accept responsibility or to account for one's actions.

There was a popular business book written by Jim Collins titled *Good to Great*. A major premise of the book was, "Get the right people on the bus, then figure out where to drive it."³ The companies selected in the book were chosen based on a strict set of measurable standards. The author's research team compared the leadership of the selected companies with parallel companies in their industry—companies not maintaining the same standards.

They found that the top leaders played a part in building those companies in such a way, there had been sustained growth over a number of years, growth that was far above the competition. As a result, they became leading companies

---

[1] *Source: Strong's Exhaustive Concordance # 3129; Merriam-Webster Online Dictionary. 2008.*

[2] *Source: Merriam-Webster Online Dictionary. 2008.*
[3] *Source: jimcollins.com-Good to Great*

within their respected industries. The sustained growth was not the result of just one leader, but a team of leaders. The success of those companies did not falter when top leadership passed the mantle to the next generation of leadership. The men and women under them had benefited from their years of experience and were prepared to mirror their success.

Counsel is always a two-way street; positive growth occurs as senior leaders begin pouring into junior leaders.

- Senior leaders *mirror positive characteristics* that lead to the success of the organization.
- Senior leaders *share their valuable experience* as they mentor younger leaders.
- Senior leaders share company principles while holding *younger leaders accountable to learn the material through an interactive environment.*

Through this process, change happens, and there is a continual benefit: lives are transformed leading to greatness, and the company prospers long-term.

- Team members open up and share their thoughts, and new ideas emerge resulting in *a culture of trust.*
- *Leaders become stronger* by reviewing what they have already learned and gain new insight from those they are teaching.
- *Results in transformational power* in each individual, leading him or her to greatness, which contributes to the ongoing success of the company.

In a previous book, *Freedom from S.I.N.*, I showed how spiritual principles work in a secular environment, whether the secular environment acknowledges the spiritual nature of the principles or not. With that assumption, in the following chapters, we will put these basic training principles and their corresponding positive results in spiritual terms. We will then process them through our definition of the *Mirror Principle:*

> Our current spiritual state expressed by our reflection in the mirror and our reflection to those around us.

By doing so, we will learn how important they become in any training, mentoring, or discipleship process.

CHAPTER I
MIRROR: POSITIVE REFLECTION

Christ is reflected as we gain a deeper revelation of the victory over sin.

We reflect Christ's character so others have a model to live by.

THE VICTORY OVER SIN

It was a clear day, not a cloud in the sky. The young boy was sitting by the river's edge, gazing into the water, and making faces. Each time, a new face peered back at him. Suddenly, there was a stirring in the water, and a fish jumped into the air. Startled, the boy fell backward. Laughing, he thought, "That fish scared the daylights out of me." As he regained his composure, the boy returned to his solitude, peering back over the bank only to find his image was no longer visible.

The fish stirring the silt on the bottom broke the mirror, thereby no longer allowing his image to appear. Frustrated, the boy waited for hours, or so it seemed, for the water to clear. Finally, giving up, he went about his business.

Years later, now a grown man, he returned to the river's edge. He reflected upon that clear day when he had gazed into the water making faces. It was a good memory, and he laughed at the thought of the jumping fish.

Once again, he peered over the edge and gazed at the smooth blue surface reflecting the sunlight behind him. Something was terribly wrong. The image peering back at him was old: the eyes were dark, the hair gray, and the face wrinkled. He closed his eyes and reopened them, hoping that what he had seen was some distortion in the water. Horror struck as the image mirrored back, the mouth now set in a frowning position.

How long had he lingered in life, content with the image of his youth? Sitting back he thought, "Could this be me?" Reality set in as he slowly backed away and ran from the river. A long time would pass before he would return and accept the image the river mirrored.

Have you had a similar experience? Personally, I gained revelation in a similar way, but in a different environment. Several years ago, while attending Church, I agreed to sit for an interview. They explained the purpose of the interview was to produce a video depicting various age groups represented among the congregation. At 50, I represented the elderly group, considering the average age of our congregation could not have been more than 26 at the time.

Upon arriving for the interview, I was instructed to take a seat in front of a dark curtain in alignment with the light and camera. I have to admit I was excited at the prospect of being included and finished the interview feeling invigorated. Several weeks passed until at last they were going to show the video. I waited eagerly to see the performance.

Shock was the only word that came to mind watching the screen. The hair on the person in the interview was gray! The thought creased my mind, "How can this be? After all I have been looking in a mirror every morning of my life." I was clueless about how gray my hair had become.

Years had seemingly passed me by. How could I have been deceived into thinking I was still young looking? After all, I felt young. From that day on, the fact would remain—I was growing older. The question then became, "Was I ready to accept the image that appeared at my river's edge?

We all go through life, our self-images seemingly intact. As the years come and go, we do not necessarily feel any older, but there will come a day when we will have to face our true reflection. Unfortunately, sin becomes the fish in our story, fogging our mirror and distorting our true reflection.

That sinful reflection makes it hard for us to believe that God has a purpose for our life. There is good news. The victory over sin is simple: embrace eternal life through Jesus Christ. We win the victory by acknowledging Christ' atoning sacrifice on the cross for our sins, putting our trust in Jesus Christ for salvation, inviting His Holy Spirit to come into our heart, and asking Him to be the Lord of our life.

> "Most assuredly, I say to you, he who hears My word and believes in Him who sent Me has everlasting life, and shall not come into judgment, but has passed from death into life.
>
> John 5:24

As we begin to see our reflection through the atoning sacrifice of Christ, we will gain a deep revelation of the victory over sin and begin to grow in our relationship with the Lord.

> He is the atoning sacrifice for our sins, and not only for ours but also for the sins of the whole world.
> 1 John 2:2 (NIV)

> And if Christ *is* in you, the body *is* dead because of sin, but the Spirit *is* life because of righteousness. But if the Spirit of Him who raised Jesus from the dead dwells in you, He who raised Christ from the dead will also give life to your mortal bodies through His Spirit who dwells in you.
> Romans 8:10-11

From that point forward, you will begin to discern the true reflected nature of your heart and will grow spiritually.

> Spiritually, when we look at our reflection through Christ, He will reveal the true nature of our heart and our sinful appearance. As in water, face reflects face, so a man's heart reveals the man.
> Proverbs 27:19

Initially, our mirror image will not look so good. We will continue to see the reflection of our inner man where sin abounds. However, now that we are victorious over that sinful nature, the Holy Spirit begins to alter our image. Life continues to be difficult, but as we persevere, we see our character: our altered reflection. We will have less stress, frustration, contention, anger, and selfishness, just to name a few.

> Therefore, having been justified by faith, we have peace with God through our Lord Jesus Christ, through whom also we have access by faith into this grace in which we stand, and rejoice in hope of the glory of God. And not only that, but we also glory in tribulations, knowing that tribulation produces perseverance; and perseverance, character; and character, hope. Now hope does not disappoint, because the love of God has been poured out in our hearts by the Holy Spirit who was given to us.
> Romans 5: 1-5

As we allow Christ to teach us, mold us, and guide us through His Word, we will begin to see His reflection in ours. With sin removed, others see the change the Lord has brought about, and His light shines in their darkness. He has performed plastic surgery on us in a spiritual sense.

> But we all, with unveiled face, beholding as in a mirror the glory of the Lord, are being transformed into the same image from glory to glory, just as by the Spirit of the Lord.
> 2 Corinthians 3:18

The Mirror Principle

> [4]The Greek word for mirror in this scripture is *katoptrizomal*: To mirror oneself, to see reflected behold as in a glass.

Don't you find it interesting the bible refers to mirrors and reflected images? Could it be that God, knowing in our vanity we love to look at ourselves, did so for a reason?

There was a time, like the boy in my story, that the only way you could see your reflection would be to look in a stream, a piece of metal, or some other reflective material. Incredibly, through technology today we can create mirrors that produce a near perfect image. Texas Instruments, located in Dallas, Texas, has used mirrors to create a near perfect projected image. They have borrowed from the Lord's technology and are using it in incredible ways.

> [5]The DLP® chip is probably the world's most sophisticated light switch. It contains a rectangular array of up to 2 million hinge-mounted microscopic mirrors; each of these micro mirrors measures less than one-fifth the width of a human hair. When a DLP® chip is coordinated with a digital video or graphic signal, a light source, and a projection lens, its mirrors can reflect a digital image onto a screen or other surface. The DLP® chip and the sophisticated electronics that surround it are what we call DLP® technology.

---

[4] *Source: #2734 Strong's Exhaustive Concordance of the Bible; Copyright, 1980 by James Strong, Madison, N.J.*
[5] *Source: http://www.dlp.com/tech/what.aspx*

When you look in your mirror, whom do you see? Do you recognize the person peering back at you? Are you content with this person? Is the person you are looking at the same person other people see when they come face to face with you? What is the spiritual condition of the person looking back at you?

Reflecting Christ's Character

Think for a moment about a person extremely burned, and after being treated, their face is bandaged and no longer visible. Would it be correct to assume that when the doctor takes the bandages off for the first time, the person will request a mirror? After all, who could blame them?

Obviously, this person would have a fearful right to see if their face had healed from the burns. The reflected image could very well result in or have an effect on his internal perspective. However, would the image that appeared in the mirror really alter who he was on the inside?

We have all experienced difficulties. However, the reality of life is that we are who we are, regardless if we are looking in a mirror or staring off into space. How have the burns of your life experiences affected your reflection?

Realistically, when we trust Christ for salvation, we are not going to get up the next day, look in the mirror, and see an immediate change. However, over time, the change in our inner appearance will become evident to those around us by our outer reflection.

One day, I met two friends I had not seen for years for lunch. We had attended the same church years earlier. As we were having lunch and catching up, one of them looked over and said, "You know you have really changed—I sense a peace about you." I found his comment interesting, and to be truthful, a part of me wanted to take offense, yes a part of me wanted to say, "Wow, didn't I have a peace about me years ago when we attended church together?"

Several years earlier, I thought I was in a good place. However, I had no idea the internal surgery the Lord was about to perform in my life. The friend testified to the fact that the Lord's surgery had an identifiable cosmetic effect on my life. Even though I had not fully embraced the change brought about in my life, the change was evident to others. I had been refined by the Lord. Instead of looking back and questioning his response, I should have been saying, "Thank you Lord for refining me in such a way that it reflects a positive image."

Of course, the process of our refinement will continue until the day we join the Lord in heaven. The changes in our lives, good or bad, will always reflect onto others. Just like the friend who said I had a peace about me, my peace, had reflected onto him.

If we pull out our old photographs and reflect, we could easily see the outward changes that have taken place over time. However, the Lord brings an inward change, a change in our heart. This inward change generates an outward reflection of Christ. One would hope, our reflection, would provide a model for others to live by.

I want to challenge you to look at your reflection in the mirror and focus on what is different.

Mirror: Positive Reflection

- Do you see the change that has taken place over the years?
- If so, what caused those changes?
- Was it just the natural aging process, or have your life experiences had an effect on the process?
- How have you reacted to the influences that the Lord has used to enact the changes in your reflection?
- What reflection do others see?
- Is your reflection empowering others to change?

I am not referring to a reflection of someone who has endured a catastrophic event like the burn victim in the earlier example, but I could be talking about his or her reaction to that event. Your current reflection is determined by life's experiences. Life will always be full of struggles and different circumstances. Our reaction to those struggles and circumstances determines our spiritual countenance.

For example, look back at the reflection of our past presidents before and after their terms in office. Look at their eyes; they speak volumes about the wear and tear brought about by the stress the position commands. Our mirror image, tells the world volumes about our lives and the stress therein.

- What is the reflection from our nation's history?
- Are we mirroring the positive aspects of that history and discarding the negative?
- What is the reflection mirrored as a result of our personal life experiences?
- Are we reflecting positive examples propelling future generations to greatness?

- If not, what reflected image is being projected to future generations?
- Does that reflection solidify our foundational structure?
- Are we reflecting the biblical standards necessary and paramount to the spiritual success of our nation?
- Are we reflecting the biblical standards necessary and paramount to the spiritual success of our families?

Our life experiences and our reaction to those experiences will reflect on those around us. In a similar way, when God calls us into relationship with people who have put their trust in Christ, we experience Christ's reflection through those individuals. Therefore, in training, mentoring, or discipleship relationships when one person takes another person under his or her wing, the goal of that relationship should be, "Lord we want to look like you, and we want to see your image reflected in each other."

I used to joke that as long as my self-image and my mirror image did not line up, I would never grow old. However, as stated earlier, watching the video at church, the self-image and the mirror image lined up pretty quickly. There was no escaping the reality—my hair had turned gray. We can no more hide from our reflection in a mirror than we can hide from the reflection of our heart.

God knows us intimately on a level we cannot possibly comprehend. We have all been created in God's image; therefore, we have the very nature of God within us. However, most of us do not allow ourselves to seek Him out, but rather we ignore His nature. The Lord knows the heart, and the heart reflects who we really are on the inside.

Does this scare you just a little? It should because you cannot hide your reflection from the Lord. Oh, you can try to hide it from your peers, you can try to hide it from your family, and you can even try to hide it from yourself, but you most definitely cannot hide it from God.

When we attempt to hide our shortcomings, we are deceived, ignorantly thinking that somehow it will protect us or make us stronger. However, as we share our experiences openly with the intention of helping others, we release the Lord's power and in turn receive a blessing.

> But be doers of the word, and not hearers only, deceiving yourselves. For if anyone is a hearer of the word and not a doer, he is like a man observing his natural face in a mirror; for he observes himself, goes away, and immediately forgets what kind of man he was. He who looks into the perfect law of liberty and continues in it, and is not a forgetful hearer but a doer of the work, this one will be blessed in what he does.
>
> James 1:22-25

To build unity and integrity in relationships, leaders must mirror the character of Christ by imparting to others what they have learned. If not, they selfishly run the risk of failure, stagnation and possibly division. In the following passage, Jesus gives us a clear directive and the benefits to be gained by dying to self.

> Then Jesus said to His disciples, "If anyone desires to come after Me, let him deny himself, and take up his

> cross, and follow Me. For whoever desires to save his life will lose it, but whoever loses his life for My sake will find it. For what profit is it to a man if he gains the whole world, and loses his own soul? Or what will a man give in exchange for his soul? For the Son of Man will come in the glory of His Father with His angels, and then He will reward each according to his works."
>
> Matthew 16:24-27

God wants to remove all our shortcomings and mold us into His image. Over time, as our relationship with Christ strengthens, we look in the mirror and see ourselves as God sees us, thereby setting a proper example for the men and women, we are to steward on life's journey. Our counsel and direction become reflections of Christ's love.

> Beloved, now we are children of God; and it has not yet been revealed what we shall be, but we know that when He is revealed, we shall be like Him, for we shall see Him as He is.
>
> 1 John 3:2

CHAPTER II
EXPERIENCE: GUIDANCE

Our experiential knowledge forms the foundation for our instruction acting as a mirror to others.

Our experiences become the guide maps for others on life's journey.

EXPERIENTIAL KNOWLEDGE

There is an old adage, "Misery loves company." When we are called to steward God's disciples, we are chosen because experientially we are qualified to speak into their life. We have labored through similar struggles and have emerged a stronger individual.

There is a newfound freedom when you come to the realization that your painful experiences have been molded by Christ into powerful testimonies. He uses us as vessels to pour out those testimonies on the people around us in order to enact an eternal transformation in their hearts. It is one thing to speak into another person's life based on our intellectual knowledge; however, when we have experience to add to our knowledge, there is spiritual power in that counsel.

God came down from Heaven and became one of us in the flesh to be a propitiation for our sins. In order to redeem us He had to endure every temptation of sin. Thus, from before the time of His death and beyond, He relates to humankind experientially.

> In this is love, not that we loved God, but that He loved us and sent His Son to be the propitiation for our sins.
> 1 John 4:10

> For we do not have a High Priest who cannot sympathize with our weaknesses, but was in all points tempted as we are, yet without sin.
> Hebrews 4:15

When we read His Word, there should be no doubt that He understands our struggles in life; thus, it makes sense that God would place people in our lives with similar experiences to provide biblical counsel. We benefit by drawing on those experiences, that are similar to those we have encountered or will encounter. Knowing they have experienced what we are going through should help us develop a confidence and inner peace that they are spiritually qualified to speak into our lives.

Surely, you would feel more comfortable if the people instructing you in life and the truths of the bible have similar experiences to go along with their head or book knowledge.

Of course, one would also hope the people instructing you were not participating in willful sin, but were reflecting Christ's image by "Walking their talk." Let's look at the qualifications for a Deacon given in 1Timothy 3:8-9.

> Likewise deacons must be reverent, not double-tongued, not given to much wine, not greedy for money, holding the mystery of the faith with a pure conscience.
>
> 1Timothy 3:8-9

The word for deacon used in first Timothy is *Diakonos*.

> [6]Diakonos - *dee-ak'-on-os* probably from an obsolete diako; an attendant, i.e. a waiter (at table or in other menial duties); specially, a Christian teacher and pastor (technically, a deacon or deaconess):—deacon, minister, servant.

The word deacon translated in Greek meant to be an attendant, servant, or minister. The definition does not just apply to church leadership, but should challenge each of us to be set apart for service, especially when speaking into the lives of those around us. The mirror image of those qualified should be a reflection of first Timothy.

Whether in school, business or life in general, we must all be led, trained, and molded in order to be smarter, better, and more productive. There are numerous societal influ-

---

[6]*Source: #1249 Strong's Exhaustive Concordance of the Bible; Copyright, 1980 by James Strong, Madison, N.J.*

ences, some positive, some negative, and we are impacted by those influences whether we want to be our not.

When a child is born into the world, do we just let the baby come out of the womb, plop on the floor, and then leave it to fend for itself? No—we nurse, protect, and care for the baby. Eventually we teach the child to walk, talk, and to reason. For the most part, our methods of instruction are inherent, each one of us have gone through the development process. We have our experiences to draw from. One would hope those experiences have prepared us to be good stewards over the lives of our children.

When a parent makes the decision to birth children, they take on a God ordained responsibility to raise those children. The same is true as we progress through the educational system. In time, we use that education to our advantage in order to be successful and live better lives. We can better relate to those coming after us who have yet to complete their education.

When people make the decision to teach, they draw from their own educational experience along with what they have learned intellectually. Their experiences will help them to be better qualified. When teachers take an oath, they do so with the responsibility to teach their students to the best of their ability.

When called to enter into relationship through discipleship, God chooses us based on the sincerity of our heart, the depth of our biblical knowledge, and the experiences of our spiritual journey. When we share with others through discipleship, we have a responsibility to steward them through life passing on what we have learned experientially and intellectually. We are all going to be held accountable by the Lord to the extent that we fulfill these missions.

> My brethren, let not many of you become teachers, knowing that we shall receive a stricter judgment.
> James 3:1

We must never assume just because we have been qualified to parent, teach, or disciple that we are somehow better or above those we parent, teach or disciple. We are all God's children, disciples of the Lord Jesus Christ, not disciples of each other. When we submit to His Lordship in the relationship, we are spiritually covered.

> For there are many insubordinate, both idle talkers and deceivers, especially those of the circumcision, whose mouths must be stopped, who subvert whole households, teaching things which they ought not, for the sake of dishonest gain.
> Titus 1:10-11

We are protected from the enemy who is out to disqualify us. We need to be on the alert because our adversary, the devil, working through our sinful nature, will attempt to keep us out of those relationships. He will tell you that your life is hard enough without taking on the problems of others. He will try to convince you that it is none of your business to speak into their lives. He may attempt you to think selfishly, "I do not have the time."

We see the result of the enemy's lies played out on a daily basis when people question our involvement in other people's lives by saying, "Who are you to instruct them? What right do you have to tell them what to do? Who do you think you are, exercising your authority over their world? After all, they should be allowed to make their own decisions."

These excuses ultimately lead to hardship within our communities. We have heard the horror stories of parents abandoning their children for whatever reason. History has shown the impact abandonment has had on those lives: hardship stretching well into adulthood and resulting in depressed feelings and unhealthy relationships.

However, when we impart spiritual knowledge based on our experiences, a new foundation can be formed. This foundation will negate the lies of the enemy and mirror hope and prosperity.

EXPERIENCE BASED GUIDE MAPS

Through discipleship, we learn to break free of negative feelings and experience healing accomplished by having another person help us sort through our past experiences with the proper perspective. We grow as they stand with us during critical times, as we bounce ideas off them, and as they assist us with major decisions in order to guide us through life.

We mature spiritually when we allow someone to look us in the eye and ask the tough questions regarding our character. Yes, when God puts two people together in this type of relationship, you both become stronger as long as you remain committed to the relationship.

These relationships consist of listening to one another, praying together for wisdom and direction, and sharing each other's life experiences. When you share those experiences, God reveals that you are not that different and that you are no better or worse than your fellow man, just in a different time zone with respect to your journey.

Through this process, we are able to develop a God directed course of action that propels each of us on our spiritual journey. Satan knows the freedom and power that results when we enter into Godly relationships that are experientially grounded. However, much to Satan's dismay, God understands Satan's evil intention, so he set a wonderful example for us to follow in the bible as He raised His own Son, Jesus Christ. He surrounded Jesus with loving parents and instructed him through Godly men and women.

> And the Child grew and became strong in spirit, filled with wisdom; and the grace of God was upon Him. His parents went to Jerusalem every year at the Feast of the Passover. And when He was twelve years old, they went up to Jerusalem according to the custom of the feast. When they had finished the days, as they returned, the Boy Jesus lingered behind in Jerusalem. And Joseph and His mother did not know it; but supposing Him to have been in the company, they went a day's journey, and sought Him among their relatives and acquaintances. So when they did not find Him, they returned to Jerusalem, seeking Him. Now so it was that after three days they found Him in the temple, sitting in the midst of the teachers, both listening to them and asking them questions. And all who heard Him were astonished at His un-

derstanding and answers. So when they saw Him, they were amazed; and His mother said to Him, "Son, why have You done this to us? Look, Your father and I have sought You anxiously." And He said to them, "Why did you seek Me? Did you not know that I must be about My Father's business?"

Luke 2:40-49

Christ was only twelve years old at the time. The Greek word used for teacher in this passage is *Didaskalos*, an instructor.

> [7]Didaskalos—an instructor (gen. or spec.): doctor, master, teacher

Jesus was sitting in the midst of the doctors, masters, and teachers, listening and asking them questions. These people were educated and experienced. Jesus was experiencing life, just as we do, and, therefore, can identify with our struggles. He desires that we overcome those struggles in order to stay on the correct path in life. There are far too many influences of sin lingering, just waiting to lure us into their clutches and pull us off the path of righteousness.

Why do you think there are so many references to sheep and their shepherds in the bible? Sheep are not intelligent animals; they flock together and follow their shepherd because they know the shepherd's voice. Sheep have no means of protecting themselves. If they wander from the herd, they run the risk of attack. Through experience, the shepherd knows there are predators lurking ready to pounce on any

---

[7]Source: # G1320, *Strong's Exhaustive Concordance of the Bible*

lone sheep in order to devour them. He is careful to keep the flock together and will always pursue strays.

> My sheep hear my voice, and I know them, and they follow me.
>
> John 10:27

> "What man of you, having a hundred sheep, if he loses one of them, does not leave the ninety-nine in the wilderness, and go after the one which is lost until he finds it?
>
> Luke 15:4

Like sheep, when we pull ourselves out of the flock, we are exposed to the attacks of life. The predator is lurking and waiting to devour us. The burdens in life are intent on bringing division, thus when we wander from the family, church, or our relationship with other Christians, we become more vulnerable to attack.

Did you see the movie *Gladiator* starring Russell Crowe? We all love movies where the hero is strong, handsome, and seemingly indestructible. Crowe's character, General Maximus Decimus Meridias, was just that.

Through the course of a treasonous event by the King's son, Maximus is stripped of his rank and the order is given to have him executed. He learns Roman soldiers are being sent to murder his wife and child. Maximus is then taken to a remote area in the forest by several of the King's men with orders to kill him. As they prepare to execute him, Maximus outwits and kills each one of them. In the fight, he sustains a deep wound, but regardless of it, he mounts a horse and rides nonstop to his home in hopes of rescuing his family.

Unfortunately, upon his arrival, he finds his wife and child hanging, seemingly burned alive. Having lost a lot of blood, he collapses exhausted; when he awakes, he is lying on a cart, his wounds being nursed by Juba, an African slave. They are being taken to market by Bedouin slave traders, where Maximus and Juba are both purchased by Proximo, a former gladiator.

Proximo owns a stable of gladiators and uses them to fight for profit at the provincial coliseums. He forces Maximus and Juba to train along with others before entering them into the competitions. Maximus, drawing from his experiences on the battlefield, soon becomes the best, and his reputation spreads throughout the region.

Proximo learns there is a new King in Rome who is preparing to host a marathon of games in the main coliseum. He has been invited to participate. Proximo calls for Maximus to join him in his quarters and a conversation ensues, where we learn that Proximo had once been a gladiator. He informs Maximus that he was granted freedom by the former King because he was victorious in the coliseum. He tells Maximus he too can gain his freedom by performing in like fashion before the people of Rome. Of course, unknown to Proximo, Maximus sees the games as an opportunity to avenge his family.

Upon their arrival in Rome, Maximus and his team of gladiators are thrust into the center of the arena. They learn for the first time that they are to play the role of the barbarian horde in a reenactment of the fall of Carthage. Suddenly, gates at one end of the arena open, and the announcer introduces the Legionnaires of Scipio Africanus, the best soldiers Rome has to offer. Prepared to attack and riding two to a chariot, they race toward the gladiators.

Maximus immediately draws from his experience on the battlefield and instructs everyone to stay close. He tells them that if they stay together, they stand a better chance of survival. Of course, several of the gladiators ignore his counsel and rush forward. Unfortunately, in their isolated state, they are picked off one by one by the enemy.

However, those that heeded his advice and huddled together remained safe. They were in a better position to mount an offensive. Each learned a valuable lesson that not only saved their lives, but also led them to victory. It was not because the gladiators standing next to them were stronger, but that *they were stronger when they remained together—unified.*

Today, our world is a lot like that arena. We are under attack from life's circumstances, much of which is rooted in our past. We need strong men and women to come along side of us and instruct us. We need them to speak to us out of their experiences and biblical knowledge in order to guide us through life. We, too, become stronger when we stay together and draw from each other's talents and gifts.

When you join with other believers through discipleship, you experience a covering. As you walk with one another fighting life's battles, you gain a respect and trust for one another. There is spiritual power in those relationships. As God brings us together, we gain a better understanding of His character and His plan for our lives, all for His glory.

If anyone speaks, let him speak as the oracles of God. If anyone ministers, let him do it as with the ability which God supplies, that in all things God may be glorified through Jesus Christ, to whom belong the glory and the dominion forever and ever. Amen
1 Peter 4:11

Therefore, whatever you want men to do to you, do also to them, for this is the Law and the Prophets.
Matthew 7:12

CHAPTER III
INTERACTION: ACCOUNTABILITY & TRUST

We mirror the gospel and hold others accountable to biblical principles in an interactive environment.

The gospel opens our minds to new revelation creating an atmosphere of trust where life issues are shared freely without apprehension.

Our masks come off, and our true reflection shines forth.

ACCOUNTABILITY THROUGH INTERACTION

It was the summer of 1971, two friends and I embarked on a road trip to the Smoky Mountain National Forest for a week of camping. We drove non-stop to Gatlinburg, Tennessee, where we loaded up on supplies before heading into the forest. We had secured a permit for a remote camping site and drove to the parking area where we would begin our journey. However, as we unloaded our gear, we realized we had forgotten batteries.

Two of us backtracked to town to purchase the batteries, while our other friend remained behind with the gear. Upon our arrival in town, we did a little exploring and time got away from us. Dusk was approaching so we started back to be reunited with our friend. However, we failed to realize that in the forest, darkness descended much earlier than in the city, and when we returned, our friend was nowhere in sight.

Having heard all the stories about bears rummaging around campsites, our friend, scared to death, had taken refuge behind a tree. Though glad to see us, he was rather upset to say the least. We learned the forest could be an intimidating environment in the absence of light.

Most of us have heard the phrase, "They couldn't see the forest for the trees." The trees of life can be big and overwhelming. Oftentimes, they shield our view, throwing us off our path in life. If you have ever spent time in the woods then you know what we experienced is true. Darkness shrouds the forest quicker than usual. The only light is the moon breaking through the treetops, assuming there is a moon. With visibility being limited, the forest becomes a completely new environment. With no means to navigate through the forest, we can become lost and frustrated.

When we interact with another in a healthy relationship through discipleship, in essence, we have someone hovering over our emotional forest. They are able to instruct us and hold us accountable to biblical principles so we do not bump into the trees of life.

Imagine for a moment, it was you in that forest and that you had became lost deep within with no means of navigation. Darkness had descended, and your visibility was zero. Suddenly, a helicopter appeared hovering overhead shining a spotlight on you, and someone began to speak via loudspeaker—the voice telling you which direction to go, warning you every time you were about to hit a tree. Would their voice bring comfort and a sense of relief? Of course, with confidence restored there would be renewed hope that you would eventually find your way through the forest.

Have you ever had an experience in life where you failed to heed the voice of counsel? If you are like most of us, at some point, you have not heeded instruction and paid a major consequence as a result. Yes, it is like a voice telling us to go right, but we still long to go left and "Pow," we hit a tree. The voice then says, "I told you to go right." Again, the voice speaks and tells us to go right, but we insist on going left, and "Pow," we hit another tree. Eventually, the pain hurts so much we take a step back and reevaluate our path. It then makes sense to heed the counsel.

As a result of heeding the counsel, our lives become more manageable, and we reach our intended destination. Our willingness to listen and respond will also contribute to a healthier interaction between you and the person offering the counsel. God provides a way out of our forests in life. He will intervene to guide us through life's issues.

> The God of this people Israel chose our fathers, and exalted the people when they dwelt as strangers in the land of Egypt, and with an uplifted arm He brought them out of it.
>
> Acts 13:17

We all need someone to instruct us, encourage us, and hold us accountable as we grow and mature along our spiritual journey. The goal is to learn from them by mirroring their counsel and following their example. If we remain open to those people God puts in our paths, we realize it is the Lord hovering above our forest guiding us. We are steered to the right and to the left until one day, we look up and find ourselves in a beautiful meadow, behind us, the forest of issues from which we emerged.

The forest serves as a reminder of where we have been, but in the eternal perspective, our forest experiences are short lived. When the victory has been tasted, we no longer dwell on the pain of the journey. In fact, we are given the opportunity to share those forest experiences with others, at which time we realize that by sharing our experiences we are able to help them on their journey through life.

The challenge in life on this side of eternity is the willingness to keep re-entering the forests of life, knowing that God will direct our paths. God is our ultimate covering and provides an example how to live our life. He created us in His image and loved us so much that He gave His only begotten Son to bear the burden for our sins.

> For God so loved the world that He gave His only begotten Son, that whoever believes in Him should not perish but have everlasting life.
> John 3:16

He longs to have relationship with each of us, and through His word, He reveals His love and plan for our lives. There are thirty-one chapters in the book of Proverbs, one for every day of the month. These verses can be likened to the helicopters hovering over our emotional forest and guiding us by the light of God's wisdom and understanding.

Proverbs speak to us about the importance of the mother and the father, who we should spend time with, and who we should avoid and provides guidelines for living.

> The proverbs of Solomon the son of David, king of Israel: To know wisdom and instruction, To perceive the words of understanding, To receive the instruction of wisdom, Justice, judgment, and equity; To give prudence to the simple, To the young man knowledge and discretion—A wise *man* will hear and increase learning, And a man of understanding will attain wise counsel, To understand a proverb and an enigma, The words of the wise and their riddles. The fear of the LORD *is* the beginning of knowledge, *But* fools despise wisdom and instruction.
> Proverbs 1:1-7

For this reason, it is so important for us to enter into healthy relationships that are interactive, where we hold each other accountable to the Lord's instruction. Iron sharpens iron. We sharpen one another by sharing the word of truth as expressed in the bible and by our example. Christ reflected in our daily living.

> As iron sharpens iron, So a man sharpens the countenance of his friend.
> Proverbs 27:17

Atmosphere of Trust

Building an atmosphere of trust takes time, and we must feel comfortable with the people we let into our lives. It is the same if we are talking about a personal, business, or educational setting. The people we surround ourselves with will affect us in either a positive way or negative way. Positive role models make the difference in setting our future course in life. When genuine care is conveyed, through loving counsel or instruction, everyone benefits.

When considering an accountability or mentoring partner, you want to seek the Lord's direction. He will bring people who can relate to your issues, but who are not caught up in the emotions of your issues. Here are several points for consideration:

- What is their spiritual belief system?
- What is their testimony?
- Do they have anything to gain materially by spending time with you?
- Are they exhibiting biblical integrity?
- Are they being held accountable for their actions?
- What fruit is being produced in and through them?
- Are they participating in any habitual sin?

Many will give the right answers to our questions, but if they are hiding some form of sin or if they are a negative influence, they will be putting you at risk.

Let us look at a couple of secular examples to support this point. You just joined a new company, and one of the tenured executives offers to mentor you. You would naturally expect the person to be knowledgeable and assume he or she was a person of integrity. Thus, it would make sense to learn everything this person had to offer and mirror his or her behavior in order to be successful.

What if you later discovered the person mentoring you was embezzling funds and that others within the organization were suspicious? Would you want to mirror that behavior as well? How will the person's reputation affect the perception other employees have of you? Would they warmly embrace you?

Take another example: the education of our children. Today the quality of our public educational system is at an all time low. Assume there are two types of instructors who are going to teach and hold our students accountable. First, the positive role model and second the negative role model.

- The positive role model—a teacher who shows up on time and has lesson plans prepared. The teacher that structures time effectively and has an accountability system in place. Each student knowing his or her status on an ongoing basis. The positive role model consistently mirrors the proper moral and ethical behavior outside the classroom. Their students are impacted in a positive manner.

- The negative role model—a teacher who shows up late and has a limited or is lacking a lesson plan. The teacher has no structure in place to hold students accountable. The negative role model says one thing in the classroom, but exhibits a contradictory behavior and lifestyle outside the classroom. The students under them impacted in a negative manner.

Which would you choose for your child? What will be the long-term impact on the students under the positive role model? What will be the long-term impact on the students under the negative role model?

Whether the teaching is positive or negative, there will be an impartation of knowledge. I think we would agree that we would prefer the delivery from the positive role model, especially when it comes to our own children.

Think back on your own life experience. Was there someone who had a positive impact and made a difference in your life? Was there someone who had a negative impact on your life?

It has been a while since I attended college, but I still remember the professors who had the most impact on my life. Thinking back, three quickly come to mind (names will be omitted to protect the innocent).

The first was an English professor. Because of a physical defect she had, each day, we constructed a stage at the front of the classroom so she would be elevated to deliver her lecture. She afforded us creative ability and encouraged us to write about any of our experiences. She allowed us to share what was on our minds and to talk openly about those experiences. The class was fun and interactive. We could not wait to attend, and few ever thought about skipping her class. We did not want to miss anything, but more importantly, we did not want to let her down. She gained our respect and trust because she was not only prepared, but also held us accountable, thereby showing she truly cared.

The next professor who comes to mind taught history. He brought history to life in the classroom. He was organized and covered the material in such a way that time seemed to stand still. He also knew how to challenge his students and hold them accountable. He required that we learn everything covered in class as well as the material in the book. For that reason, few dared to miss his class. Because of his enthusiasm and methods, I still enjoy studying history.

The third person was an organic chemistry professor. His accent was so heavy that no one could understand him. He would quickly enter the classroom, rush through his notes, and exit. Not once did he offer to assist us with our questions about the material. Most of us struggled all semester with that course. It turns out that he was more interested in his research; teaching was something he had to do. The unfortunate thing about his class was the negative impact it had on so many students.

Therefore, a major key to building an atmosphere of trust is to surround yourself with positive role models as you walk the path of life.

OUR MASKS COME OFF

Several years ago, I was visiting with a friend who was reflecting on his behavior in various situations. He related how at times he acted arrogantly. The behavior manifested when he was discussing topics where he was more knowledgeable than the other person. He went on to say it was really a cover-up; he was feeling insecure and having more knowledge made him feel important. He was masking his true feelings.

Most of us are familiar Leonardo DiCaprio's role as the King in the movie *Man with an Iron Mask*, prisoner 6438900. The musketeers are committed protectors of the crown. Their motto "One for all and all for one" was famous, as was their reputation in France at the time.

The King, Louie the XIV, was a ruthless ruler, allowing his people to starve by storing all the available food for his army. The Jesuit Priests had plotted to kill him, and many attempts were made on the King's life. To combat these attacks, Louie recruits one of the retired Musketeers, Aramis, also a priest, to locate and kill the General of the Jesuit Order. What the King does not know is that Aramis is the General of the Jesuit Order.

Obviously alarmed by the King's request, Aramis calls a meeting of three of the most revered musketeers, Athos, Porthos, and D'Artagnan. Athos and Porthos are retired, but D'Artagnan is still in the King's service and is, in fact, the King's number one bodyguard. Aramis reveals the King's intention. Aramis confesses to his fellow musketeers that he is the General of the Jesuit Order.

He suggests they employ their own plan to thwart the evil King. We soon learn his plan is to use an imprisoned man wearing an iron mask to impersonate the King. You will have to watch the movie to see how they break this man out of prison.

Successful in their plan to rescue the man, they remove the mask and have him cleaned up and dressed. Joining the musketeers, he is seated at the head of a large table. Athos,

Porthos, and D'Artagnan are astonished. He looks identical to the King.

We learn his name is Philippe, and six years earlier, he had been living an obscure life on a country estate. One day a man in black representing the King showed up and took him to the prison, where he was fitted with the iron mask. His only thought at the time was it must have had something to do with his face. Aramis then says something deeply profound to Philippe, "*The greatest mystery of life is who we truly are.*"

I relate this movie for a reason: we all wear masks at one time or another. Some of us are well aware of our masks, but many of us are not. Regardless of whether we wear them knowingly or unknowingly, *they hide who we are on the inside* and give others a false perception of our true nature.

We don some masks thinking they will protect us and other masks thinking they will empower us. Either way, these masks cause us to project behaviors contrary to who we really are on the inside. When we wear these masks, we become deceived about our heart's true identity. When we look in the mirror, all we see is the mask; we do not see the inner person that God created under the mask.

Another movie helps us to grasp this reality. The movie with Jim Carrey aptly titled *The Mask*. Carrey plays a young man distraught with life, a life void of excitement, until one day he happens upon an ancient mask. He takes the mask home and standing in front of his mirror, slowly lifts the mask to his face. Suddenly, like a magnet, the mask attaches itself to him. Immediately, he enters into a trance-like state and in a literal whirlwind transforms into a slick, slippery, bold, and seductive character: his alter ego.

Everything he lacked in the natural, the man in the mask personified with perfection. Nothing and no one could stop him, and everyone was drawn to him. As long as the young man was wearing the mask, he was confident and indestructible, but as soon as the mask came off, he returned to his normal state, drained and even more confused.

Like my friend dealing with his arrogance, there are times when our sinful nature rises up, and we put on an invisible mask. For some, it might be a mask of power and dominance, and for others it is a mask of burden and depression. Some have closets full of masks from which to choose. Regardless, in doing so, we activate our sin nature, and those around us get a distorted vision of who we really are.

How many people do you know who have altered their natural state through plastic surgery? Just open any magazine and look at the advertisements: plastic surgery, breast augmentation, liposuction, Botox treatments, and dental makeovers. They scream, "You don't have to look like that. We can make you beautiful, more appealing, and most importantly, feel better about yourself."

My mother returned home after a day spent with some friends and related the horror she felt when she encountered a friend who decided to have a facelift. This person was a beautiful woman to begin with. Unfortunately, because of her husband's infidelity, she felt the need to a have a facelift in hopes that she would be more attractive and appealing to him. In essence, she had donned a permanent mask in an attempt to woo her husband's affection. Unfortunately, her facelift did not keep her husband at home.

Please understand there is a need for these services, especially when correcting deformities from birth, illnesses, or accidents. Many women faced with breast cancer opt for reconstructive surgery, which is a wonderful option to help overcome the devastating emotional pain of a mastectomy. Others are born with various defects, such as the case with conjoined twins. Still others decide to enhance their looks through a healthy process. In these instances, thank God that He has put it on the hearts of men and women to study diligently and hone their medical skills in order to bring restoration to so many.

It is not the intention of this writing to debate the moral or the ethical grounds of plastic surgery. The point I am making is that many people are using surgical masks as a means of escaping their true identity. As a result, the cosmetic surgery industry is thriving.

Of course, you remember Michael Jackson, how he captured everyone's heart as a little boy singing with his brothers. His dance moves had a mesmerizing effect on women, young and old alike. For some unknown reason, he began to alter his looks through plastic surgery until one day he no longer resembled the person God created him to be.

Along with his new image, a new behavior developed until one day fans became confused about who was behind the mask. Michael had an incredible platform to be a positive role model. Just think what might have been if he had gained a revelation of who birthed his talent—a loving and supreme God. God provided him with a gift so incredible, which if used according to the purpose God intended, could have led millions of people toward an eternal life with Jesus Christ.

Unfortunately, he chose to don a mask, obviously discontent with who God created him to be. Michael ultimately gave in to the sin inside his heart by altering his looks.

We look at his story not to judge Michael, but rather to give thought about our own masks, some worn knowingly and some unknowingly. Many of those masks cause us pain. They are intent on our destruction and ultimate separation from our creator.

At those times, the reflection we see in the mirror is not who we really are or who we necessarily desire to be. Those who know our true nature will see through the mask and immediately know something is wrong. However, those who do not know us have no previous ground on which to judge our character. To them, the behavior is reflective of who we really are. In other words, their perception of us becomes their reality.

False perceptions are one way our spiritual enemy has turned the table on Christians. We have all heard nonbelievers state, "If that behavior or speech is an example of what being a Christian is, I don't want anything to do with being a Christian." Without knowing it, the church has donned a mask and distorted the image that they confess to build their lives on—the image of Jesus Christ. Thus, they are driving more people away from the very entity they profess to embrace.

Remember the words of Aramis, "The greatest mystery of life is who we truly are." When we look in the mirror, is it the mask we see, or do we see the real person behind the mask? If all we choose to see when we look in the mirror are the masks of life, then we are ignoring our sinful nature.

> So the LORD said to Cain, "Why are you angry? And why has your countenance fallen? If you do well, will you not be accepted? And if you do not do well, sin lies at the door. And its desire *is* for you, but you should rule over it."
> Genesis 4:6--7

No one is immune from sin's scheme; sin is like a viral strain. It disguises itself, thus making it hard to identify. In life, viral cells take on the image of the cells around them in order to deceive our systems. Sometimes, the more you try to eradicate it, the stronger it becomes. The only thing that will uncover and expose our sinful nature is the truth. Thus, until we are willing to see our true reflection, the reflection that God sees, we are deceived and subject to sin's grasp on our lives.

God will use other people to mirror and expose the deception and destruction sin imposes. He will use people who care about us, but are not tied to our emotional baggage. For that reason, they are able to see clearly those areas of life where we have become bogged down by the cares of the world. They are able to show us a reflection of the destruction that has resulted from sin. Eventually, an atmosphere of trust is established.

By the way, there is a quick fix for sin—confession of the truth.

> Confess your trespasses to one another, and pray for one another, that you may be healed. The effective, fervent prayer of a righteous man avails much.
>
> James 5:16

Why do you think we are instructed to confess one to another? Confession brings healing from the hold our sinful nature has on our inner being and allows the Holy Spirit to enter into that area of our heart and cleanse us.

Please note we want to make sure the person we are confessing to is living righteously because the "fervent prayer of a righteous man avails much." When we confess to one another through discipleship, trust is built, and we gain a sense of peace that comes only from the love of Christ. We are instructed to hear their confessions and to restore them in a spirit of gentleness. We never know when it may be our turn to confess. Temptation is always just around the corner.

> Brethren, if a man is overtaken in any trespass, you who are spiritual restore such a one in a spirit of gentleness, considering yourself lest you also be tempted.
>
> Galatians 6:1

In the 1700's, John and Charles Wesley started The Holy Club at Oxford. Once a week, Wesley and a few men met and asked each other a variety of questions pertaining to their actions the previous week. They held each other accountable to follow a righteous lifestyle.

Out of that club, the Methodist Church Movement was birthed. They had a *method* for living out the instructions in the bible. As they held each other accountable to a biblical standard, they were individually blessed. Let us take a close look at the questions John Wesley created for his group at Oxford.

1. Am I consciously or unconsciously creating the impression that I am better than I really am? In other words, am I a hypocrite?
2. Do I confidentially pass on what was told to me in confidence?
3. Can I be trusted?
4. Am I a slave to dress, friends, work, or habit?
5. Am I self-conscious, self-pitying, or self-justifying?
6. Did the Bible live in me today?
7. Do I give God time to speak to me every day?
8. Am I enjoying prayer?
9. When did I last speak to someone else of my faith?
10. Do I pray about the money I spend?
11. Do I get to bed on time and get up on time?
12. Do I disobey God in anything?
13. Do I insist on doing something about which my conscience is uneasy?
14. Am I defeated in any part of my life?
15. Am I jealous, impure, irritable, touchy, or distrustful?
16. How do I spend my spare time?
17. Am I proud?
18. Do I thank God I am not as other people, especially as the Pharisees who despised the publican?
19. Is there anyone I fear, or dislike, or criticize, or resent? If so, what am I doing about it?
20. Do I grumble or complain consistently?
21. Is Christ real to me?

Each question deals with character. I challenge you to copy this list, get up each morning, read over it, and hold yourself accountable to these questions. I guarantee you that your life will never be the same.

However, if you are like most of us, at some point, you will forget to read over the list and eventually will forget where you put the list. Human behavior is such that we are self-motivated to a point, and each person has a different discipline in that regard. We need other people to speak life to us. We enter into relationships with other people because we were not created to be alone.

> Not forsaking the assembling of ourselves together, as is the manner of some, but exhorting one another, and so much the more as you see the Day approaching.
>
> Hebrews 10:25

Through positive interaction, accountability and trust are established. These discipleship elements work in tandem, and we become disciples of those charged to teach, train, or mentor us. The more that trust is developed the better positioned we are to form positive life patterns benefiting us long-term. As we consistently show up and diligently embrace positive counsel, our lives are impacted and our eternal purposes propelled.

CHAPTER IV
Reinforce: Strength & Covering

Our walk with the Lord is reinforced becoming stronger as we teach and learn from those we are called to disciple.

We are strengthened as the spiritual instruction flows both ways.

"Umbrella Effect" Christ mirrors three primary levels of covering.

CALLED TO DISCIPLE

Church ended one Sunday, and I rushed to the front in order to catch the Pastor before everyone vied for his attention. After all, I had something important to tell him. I had an idea for a men's group, and knowing how much he enjoyed speaking into leaders lives, I had no doubt he would embrace my idea with enthusiasm.

Sure enough, I reached him first and shared my idea about starting a men's group. What happened next was unexpected. He offered a question, "How many men are you currently in a disciple relationship with?"

Caught off guard, I stuttered, saying, "Well there is ugh and there is ugh."

He interrupted the stuttering by saying, "Why don't you start by finding one person to disciple?" Our conversation ended abruptly, and I decided a conversation with the Lord was in order.

Of course, it was a one-way conversation. I was doing the talking in hopes that God was listening. Ever had one of those conversations? I told the Lord, "Okay, if you want me to disciple someone, then you bring him to me. I am not going to go select someone at random." That was pretty much the end of the conversation because the Lord did not choose to offer a response.

I cannot recall anything about the following week, what my thoughts were or my prayers. The following Sunday, I was the lead usher and arrived early to set up for the first service. One of the other ushers approached with a question, "Are you currently in a discipleship relationship with anyone?"

I responded with my own question, "Why do you ask?" I was thinking, "The Pastor must have mentioned our conversation."

However, much to my surprise he said, "Because I need someone to speak into my life, and since I've gotten to know you, I have gained a respect for the way you are living life."

I was caught off guard once again, but from a different perspective. This particular individual knew more scripture and had spent as much or more time in ministry than I had. However, because of the struggles set before him, he sought out counsel from someone who had experience. Fortunately,

Christ's reflection was evident in how I was walking out my faith. As a result, I was considered approved to speak into his life.

My only response had to be, "It would be an honor to meet with you." We set a time, and for the next three years, we were pretty faithful to meet once a week. The fruit of our meetings and the counsel offered over those three years blessed him and mirrored back a blessing to me. The counsel reinforced what I had learned and strengthened my walk with the Lord. We both benefited from the experience, and our lives were altered spiritually.

God created us to be in relationship and for that reason, something happens to us on the inside when we enter into healthy relationships. When we stand together and ask life's tough questions, we are able to embrace God's power and use that power to strengthen one another. We become stronger and more stable.

> Go therefore and make disciples of all the nations, baptizing them in the name of the Father and of the Son and of the Holy Spirit,
>
> Matthew 28:19

The Lord has commissioned us to "Go therefore and make disciples of all the nations." The Lord did not say, "If you are so inclined or when you are not fishing, why don't you go and disciple a few people?" As we can clearly see here in Matthew, discipleship is not an option for the Christian.

Spiritual Instruction Flows Both Ways

Why do you think Christ was so adamant in commissioning His Disciples? Could it possibly be to lead people into heaven and away from hell? To be sure, but shall we limit God? God also knew in the process of making disciples, His representatives would be reinforced and strengthened in their own relationship with Him.

Every time we speak experientially into the life of another person, it mirrors back to us in order to reinforce what we have learned and what we have endured. It strengthens our resolve, empowers our counsel, solidifies our faith, and helps us to remain steadfast in our goal to be like Christ. The word of God brings us revelation in various ways. Personally, when I am speaking into someone's life, I am always humbled when words not my own come out of my mouth.

Many times, I have been left thinking, "Oh, I wish I hadn't said that because now the Lord is going to hold me accountable to those words." Discipleship is not just for those we are called into relationship with; it is also for our own growth and protection. We are in a battle and will struggle with the enemy's attacks until the day the Lord takes us home to live with Him in heaven.

> Our adversary the devil walks about like a roaring lion, seeking whom he may devour
>
> 1 Peter 5:8

When God allows us to speak into another person's life, He is not going to miss an opportunity to work in and through both individuals. Remember God is

Omnipotent—He is all-powerful

> He has made the earth by His power,
> He has established the world by His wisdom,
> And has stretched out the heavens at His discretion.
> Jeremiah 10:12

Omniscient—He knows all things

> And there is no creature hidden from His sight, but all things *are* naked and open to the eyes of Him to whom we *must give* account.
> Hebrews 4:13

Omnipresent—He is everywhere at the same time

> "*Am* I a God near at hand," says the LORD, "And not a God afar off? Can anyone hide himself in secret places, So I shall not see him?" says the LORD; "Do I not fill heaven and earth?" says the LORD.
> Jeremiah 23:23-24

It makes sense that as we speak into another person's life, God will be instructing us as well. I have oft said, "If the Holy Spirit shows up, even if He is speaking through me, I had better be open to listen."

If he is using you as His instrument, it may be just as much or more for your benefit as it is to the person to whom you are speaking. In other words, as we give advice, we should take heed to put into practice that which we preach. If not, we run the risk of being disqualified.

> But I discipline my body and bring it into subjection, lest, when I have preached to others, I myself should become disqualified.
>
> 1 Corinthians 9:27

The Lord's counsel will always mirror back into our lives and reinforce that the victory over sin is His. We are strengthened in our walk with Him so that we do not fall prey to the everyday attacks of the enemy disguised in the cares of this world. The Lord is the ultimate trainer.

I challenge you to consider times when someone has given you permission to speak into his or her life. Has your counsel revealed what is in your heart? As we look in the lives of others, we can easily criticize their faults, issues and actions. However, when we speak into another's life and allow our reflection to mirror back, we see our own shortcomings as well.

> Or how can you say to your brother, 'Brother, let me remove the speck that is in your eye,' when you yourself do not see the plank that is in your own eye? Hypocrite! First remove the plank from your own eye, and then you will see clearly to remove the speck that is in your brother's eye.
>
> Luke 6:42

Our shortcomings might be manifested in a different way. Nevertheless, at our core, we are all human, subject to life's struggles. To make this point clear, you only have to reflect on a time when you corrected someone else's behavior about a certain issue, only later to be faced with a similar issue. Did you employ the same counsel?

In those times, why do we need someone to echo back to us what we have taught others? We know that it is easier to give counsel than to receive counsel. Look at your reflection in the mirror. What do you see? Is Jesus reflected in you? Are you the same on the inside as the person being reflected on the outside? What does your reflection tell you? Have you come face to face with Christ? Do you see Jesus reflected in others?

The Umbrella Effect

Consider the umbrella, unopened it offers no protection; we have only a thin cylindrical shaft. However, as we open the canopy and allow it to spread out, all are protected who remain underneath. There is but one prerequisite for covering: we must open the umbrella.

There are two truths when we remain under the Lord's covering by opening our spiritual umbrellas:

Our walk with Him will be reinforced
&
Our journey through life is strengthened

Think for a moment about a healthy company environment in which employees experience the proper covering. The company puts them through training in order to impart knowledge of the business and to equip them for the tasks they are to perform. When the company conducts periodic performance reviews, the employees are analyzed and given feedback about their performances. Goals are set, and new challenges are put in place. Employees are empowered to perform and encouraged to be all they can be.

This covering strengthens them in life. The employees are comforted every time their paychecks are deposited in their accounts. They are reassured each time they have to go to the doctor, and the company insurance helps with the bills and the many other benefits that come with the job.

These benefits are provided as long as the employees stay under accountability and respond appropriately to their superiors. If they remain true, and their superiors remain true, it is possible for them to have a long and healthy career. The umbrella is open and firmly in place.

On the contrary, think about the company in which the environment is unhealthy, and employees are not covered. Maybe the owner of the company flies by the seat of his pants, wearing all of the hats: inventor, manufacturer, salesperson, distributor, and accountant. Eventually, he makes the decision and hires several people. He then attempts to train them and watch over them to make sure business is being handled correctly. Now, he is faced with a dilemma: others are in a position to make mistakes. Given his affinity for taking on all the functions of the company, he keeps a firm grip on every area. He has trouble letting his people make decisions and begins dictating how they should run their departments.

Are his employees being strengthened in life? Unknowingly, he has closed the umbrella, no longer providing covering necessary for his employees to prosper and grow. It is only a matter of time before the employees start vacating the company.

In life, The Umbrella Effect is played out clearly in the family. We are all born into a family, and it is up to the mother and father to raise and provide for their children. The children develop and mature when they are fed, provided shelter, and receive a good education. As long as the children remain under their parents' accountability and respond respectfully to instruction, they will continue to reap the benefits of the family environment. Their lives strengthened as a result.

The same holds true in our church environments. People have the opportunity to be strengthened as they remain under the church's umbrella of spiritual covering. They have a place where they are taught the word of God, a place where they find fellowship with other believers, and a place where their kids can learn about God.

We should be thankful every time we receive from the church some form of benefit or service, such as, but not limited to, discipleship, prayer, hospital visits, marriage ceremonies, funerals, or private counsel. There are too many benefits derived from the church to list.

Unfortunately, we have people walking around our cities, umbrellas in hand, getting sopping wet with the cares of this world. In order to find strength and mature in life, one must accept the covering provided. It makes sense to enter in and remain in close relationship with other like-minded individuals. The covering these relationships bring, strengthen all parties participating in the process; everyone benefits.

Jesus Christ put the umbrella effect in motion when he mirrored three levels of covering vital to achieve and sustain the proper balance in his own life.

Christ established the first level of covering by selecting His inner circle consisting of Peter, James and John. He journeyed through life with them, teaching, laughing, and even lamenting with them. These relationships were His deepest ones spiritually while on earth. They ascended the Mount of Transfiguration where Jesus met with Moses and Elijah. These three men were with Jesus in the solitude of the garden during the final hour leading up to His arrest. He shared an intimacy with them that was different from the intimacy He shared with the other disciples.

> Then they came to a place which was named Gethsemane; and He said to His disciples, "Sit here while I pray." And He took Peter, James, and John with Him, and He began to be troubled and deeply distressed. Watch and pray, lest you enter into temptation. Verse 38, The spirit indeed is willing, but the flesh is weak."
> Mark 14:32-33, 38

> Now after six days Jesus took Peter, James, and John his brother, led them up on a high mountain by themselves; and He was transfigured before them. His face shone like the sun, and His clothes became as white as the light. And behold, Moses and Elijah appeared to them, talking with Him.
> Matthew 17:1

Christ established the second level of covering by surrounding Himself with twelve disciples, which included His inner circle of Peter, James, and John. These men experienced life with Him. They were present when He fed the five thousand, when He healed the sick, when He cast out demons, and when He brought Lazarus back to life.

Jesus appeared to them and His other disciples after His crucifixion and continued to instruct them about the kingdom of God. With the exception of Judas, who was replaced by Matthias, they became Apostles. They were His representatives here on earth, and every one of them stayed true to his commitment. In the end, all but John died a martyr's death.

> And when He had called His twelve disciples to Him, He gave them power over unclean spirits, to cast them out, and to heal all kinds of sickness and all kinds of disease. Now the names of the twelve apostles are these: first, Simon, who is called Peter, and Andrew his brother; James the son of Zebedee, and John his brother; Philip and Bartholomew; Thomas and Matthew the tax collector; James the son of Alphaeus, and Lebbaeus, whose surname was Thaddaeus; Simon the Cananite, and Judas Iscariot, who also betrayed Him.
>
> Matthew 10:1-4

> Until the day he was taken up to heaven, after giving instructions through the Holy Spirit to the apostles he had chosen. After his suffering, he showed himself to these men and gave many convincing proofs that he was alive. He appeared to them over a period of forty days and spoke about the kingdom of God.
>
> Acts 1:2-3

Christ's third level of covering was the Church. The Church represents a much broader covering in the sense that it included His inner circle, the additional nine, and other believers following Him at the time. After His resurrection, Jesus appeared to the twelve, telling them not to leave Jerusalem, but to wait for the gift of the Holy Spirit. After their arrival in Jerusalem, we learn in Acts, there were 120 disciples. It was the 120 that chose Matthias to replace Judas. These people comprised the core of the Church. They would be the first to receive the Baptism of the Holy Spirit on the day of Pentecost.

> On one occasion, while he was eating with them, he gave them this command: "Do not leave Jerusalem, but wait for the gift my Father promised, which you have heard me speak about. For John baptized with water, but in a few days you will be baptized with the Holy Spirit."
>
> Acts 1:4-5

> When the day of Pentecost came, they were all together in one place. Suddenly a sound like the blowing of a violent wind came from heaven and filled the whole house where they were sitting. They saw what seemed to be tongues of fire that separated and came to rest on each of them. All of them were filled with the Holy Spirit and began to speak in other tongues as the Spirit enabled them.
>
> Acts 2:1-4

Jesus opened His umbrella of covering and spent three years holding it over the individuals that chose to walk with

Him during that time. Today, through His word, He continues to offer His umbrella of covering and mirrors a wonderful example for us to follow.

When we join a genuine body of believers, we are in a sense given Christ's umbrella. We open the umbrella by establishing an intimate relationship with two or three others, by joining a small home group, and finally by participating in corporate worship. As we embrace the teaching and accountability provided at every level, we mirror the experience the twelve disciples enjoyed with Christ.

Through these three levels of covering, we become spiritually strong. Whether we choose to open the umbrella will be up to each one of us. Thus a good question we should all be asking is

> "Am I being challenged, reinforced, and strengthened on my spiritual journey through life?

If not, why not get your umbrella out and open it. You will begin experiencing the incredible covering Christ desires to provide all His children.

CHAPTER V
Transformation: Power & Propulsion

We are transformed by His power through the renewing of our minds.

We are propelled on life's journey as we embrace the power of the gospel.

TRANSFORMED BY THE RENEWING OF OUR MINDS

Biblical knowledge received by revelation through a right relationship with the Lord will bring transformation. By embracing the mirror principle, we begin to share in God's transformational power by the renewing of our minds. The enemy is out to silence us. He has been at work for a long time and is not ready to give up just yet. He does not want us mentoring our young and sowing seeds of truth to those around us.

> Do not conform any longer to the pattern of this world, but be transformed by the renewing of your mind. Then you will be able to test and approve what God's will is—his good, pleasing and perfect will.
> Romans 12:2

I used tell a story when my children were young about a fictional character named Prince Sam (book to follow). The stories were a lot of fun for us. However, I initially made up Prince Sam to communicate spiritual life lessons. It is important for us to sow positive biblical seed into our children's lives for the obvious reason: the seed exposes the world's lies and ultimately bears fruit, breaking sin's hold on their life.

Sin's lying spirit will always attempt to silence the spiritual instruction of the Father. To the enemy's demise, those life lessons were spiritual seeds planted in the depths of my kids' hearts.

A pastor once held up a packet of seed in front of his congregation and slowly poured some into his hand. He asked the congregation if the seed he held in his hand looked like the plants pictured on the packet. The obvious answer was no. He took the seed and threw it out at the audience. He then said, "We are called to sow our seed into the world, starting with the places we visit each and every day."

There will be times when we will become discouraged that the seed we sow may not sprout and take root. There may be times we will become discouraged when others attempt to discount the importance of our seed. However, these thoughts and reactions should not keep us from sowing the seed.

Farmers go out every year and prepare their land for the planting season. Although they have prepared their land to receive the seed, they do not know for sure if the seed is going to grow. However, because of past experience, they know that when the soil is ready and the seed is sown, it will grow. When tended to properly by adding the right amount of nutrients and providing a good water source, the seed is going to sprout and grow into whatever the intended crop is to be.

Likewise, when we sow biblical seed along with the seed of our life experiences into others, we can have confidence that those seeds will ultimately produce a bountiful crop in their lifetime.

> Then He said, "To what shall we liken the kingdom of God? Or with what parable shall we picture it? *It is* like a mustard seed which, when it is sown on the ground, is smaller than all the seeds on earth; but when it is sown, it grows up and becomes greater than all herbs, and shoots out large branches, so that the birds of the air may nest under its shade."
>
> Mark 4:30-32

The mind is a powerful organ capable of great insights and vision. By absorbing the gospel message and mirroring Christ' example, profound renewal takes place, and our lives are transformed by His power.

> For the word of God *is* living and powerful, and sharper than any two-edged sword, piercing even to the division of soul and spirit, and of joints and marrow, and is a discerner of the thoughts and intents of the heart.
>
> Hebrews 4:12

PROPELLED ON LIFE'S JOURNEY

> For I am not ashamed of the gospel of Christ, for it is the power of God to salvation for everyone who believes, for the Jew first and also for the Greek.
>
> Romans 1:16

When we share the gospel of Jesus Christ, it is His power that propels us along life's journey. The effect of His power working through us allows us to be a mirror to others, especially family and offspring.

Unfortunately, our culture dictates, "What's the point in helping others? What difference can you make? Their problems are not your responsibility. Besides you have no right to enforce your ideals on others."

The truth of the gospel brings freedom from the grasp of a spiritual enemy destined to take us to an eternity separated from our Creator. There is a reason the bible instructs us to train our children so when they are older, they "will not depart" from the truth.

> Train up a child in the way he should go, And when he is old he will not depart from it.
>
> Proverbs 22:6

School is the place where our society begins executing the mirror principle. One would hope that we are imparting the proper information and behavior for positive-growth. The reflection of that information and that process should mirror back on administrators, teachers and parents strengthening the whole system.

However, many of the liberally backed entitlement programs have attempted to silence Christ's gospel message in an attempt to weaken our foundational structures. I would like us to look at two examples, which at their core, are paramount in understanding how effective our spiritual enemy has been.

First Example

Reflect back to the year 1971. Surely, you are familiar with a concept called *bussing*. My graduation was scheduled for the year 1972, however, for many of us, the joy of our high school experience ended in 1971. The educational powers implemented a plan to bus students from one school district to another.

In theory, the concept made sense. Take a student from a lower economic background and place him in a school among students from a higher economic background; the intended result was that everyone would improve. The proponents of bussing hoped that the students being bused would be influenced by these better schools located in a more prosperous setting. I would say healthier setting, but you and I know that is not the reality. They were to take that knowledge along with a renewed hope back to their neighborhoods in order to alter their life courses.

What has history taught us as we look back at the reflection of that program? It had the reverse effect; the students resented being taken out of their neighborhoods and sent to better neighborhoods. At the end of the day, the kids from the better neighborhoods went back to their plush existence, and the kids from the poorer neighborhoods went back to their not so plush existence.

Here we are, approximately forty years, and we still have not learned our lesson. The plan that sounded so good on paper is still being mirrored within our school system. It did not work then, and it does not work now.

Hello, did anyone hear? It did not work, but for all these years, we have been chasing our tail mirroring a failed program. Now the private school sector is doing a booming business, and the schools in many neighborhoods do not reflect the populace living in those neighborhoods.

Not wanting to complain without offering a solution, let us look at a different solution. Had this solution been implemented in the 1970's in the same school district, today we might be mirroring to others one of the best public school systems in the nation. What would the reflection of the system be today if we had taken all the money spent on busing and put it into the educational process?

- Established higher standards at every level.
- Held administrators and teachers accountable to those standards based on measurable results.
- Increased educators' pay with bonuses tied to results.
- Encouraged and assisted educators in obtaining master degrees in their field of study.
- Maintained and improved all facilities including schools in the lower economic areas.
- Continued to improve on and provide the best educational tools.
- Created more extensive laboratories and libraries.
- Implemented no pass no play with zero tolerance.

Out of our ignorance, bussing lowered the overall quality of our public school system. Schools were transformed all right, but the transformation was not positive. I hope this provides some insight into how successful our spiritual enemy has been in silencing our teaching and the devastating impact it has had over time on our children.

Second Example

Let us look how the same spiritual enemy has influenced and further attacked the core foundation of our nation. The following are three of the most important professions in our society.

- Education
- Ministry
- Law enforcement

Schools exist to impart knowledge so we can learn, grow, mature, and eventually become functional members of society. Churches exist to impart biblical truth and to mirror correct behavior based on scripture in order for us to understand correct moral and ethical behavior. Law enforcement exists to enforce and hold us accountable to laws that have been set in place to provide us freedom and allow us to live in peace.

The overall impact these professions have on the foundation of our society is far greater than any other professions. The fact remains that these professions have been in place for generations in order for us to live better and more successful lives, transformed lives. They exist to help our world be a better place. However, the incomes for these vocations in the

United States are just average at best. Based on the U.S. census report published in June 2006, the following are the average earnings for these fields:

- Police officers $50,606
- Primary School Teachers $45,151
- Clergy $39,041[8]

Some folks reading this may be thinking, "These average salaries are adequate. Why aren't more people pursuing them?" To that question I challenge, "Are they sufficient to attract the best talent?" What if we could double or even triple the average salaries for these three professions? Do you think more people would be inclined to enter these professions? Do you think we might lure the best and the brightest? My guess would be a resounding yes.

To make this point clear, consider professional sports. More young people would rather play a professional sport than enter one of these three professions. The average salary for a professional athlete far exceeds those mentioned.

No one can deny sports in general are extremely important in mirroring teamwork, discipline, accountability, and goal setting; unfortunately, there is more emphasis on winning, especially at the college and university levels, where we seldom hear on a consistent basis coaches emphasizing the importance of gaining an education. Rarely, if at all, do you hear coaches bragging about the grade point averages of their players. We can easily understand why our kids would prefer to be professional athletes rather than law

---

[8] *http://www.bls.gov/ncs/ocs/sp/ncbl0910.pdf*

enforcement officers, teachers, or members of the clergy. I am not proposing that salaries should be the main motivator for choosing one of these professions. I hope people entering one of these three professions would be responding to a calling and love what they do.

There must always be balance, or greed will lure the wrong element. Unfortunately, there are other reasons besides money why people shy away from these professions.

- Teachers have to put up with disrespectful kids carrying weapons to school. They deal with government constantly interfering with the process in an attempt to dictate the content teachers are to present.

- Law enforcement officials must deal with many liberal minded individuals. These individuals have so relaxed the laws that now the felons appear to have the advantage.

- Ministry leaders have to put up with attacks from anyone and everyone who do not believe what the bible teaches. Additionally, many believers put these leaders on a pedestal. Those same criticize them if they do not live up to a certain expected standard.

Do you ever wonder who is behind the scenes causing all this negativity? We have a spiritual enemy who has been at work for years to wreak havoc on our eternal destinies. When he can weaken these three core areas, he does not have to worry about much of anything else. Transformation is stagnated.

> For we do not wrestle against flesh and blood, but against principalities, against powers, against the rulers of the darkness of this age, against spiritual *hosts* of wickedness in the heavenly places.
> Ephesians 6:12

Daily, on the news, we hear stories about kids walking into schools and churches with guns, suicide bombers, infighting between governing authorities, and division within the family. I could go on. When there is an attack on any one of these core professions, there is an attack on all three.

For instance, when there is an attack on law enforcement, people will take advantage of the system and those around them to get what they want. A good example would be the Los Angeles riots that occurred in 1992. Many people, showing no respect for law or authority, looted businesses.

When kids have no fear of retribution, there is no incentive to stay in school; thus, the entire educational system is weakened. When our educational system is weakened, so is our ability to impart knowledge and develop future leaders. Where there is ignorance, people run the risk of getting into trouble with the law.

When there is an attack on ministry, the place where people receive necessary biblical instruction, society is at risk. We lose the foundation for moral and ethical behavior. Without a moral and ethical foundation, people will not live lives of integrity, and everyone around them will suffer.

These three professions are interconnected to form a solid foundation in this country.

Reflecting on our two examples, we cannot deny there has been a focused attack at the core of our society. The principalities, powers, rulers of darkness, and the spiritual hosts of wickedness in the heavenly places knew all along that by cracking our societal foundation, they could rob God's people of biblical blessing.

However, there is hope because we have a powerful advocate in our Lord Jesus Christ who has given us His Word. The following scripture is taken from the parable of the sower in the book of Matthew, which we will look at later in closing, but for our purposes here, I ask you to focus on the numbers cited. When we embrace His teachings and guide others in wisdom tremendous fruit is produced.

> "But he who received seed on the good ground is he who hears the word and understands *it*, who indeed bears fruit and produces: some a hundredfold, some sixty, some thirty."
>
> Matthew 13:23

The parable unlocks the true nature of the gospel that will propel each of us on our life's journey. Don't you think it is time you allowed His Word to propel you on your journey?

CHAPTER VI
Trinitarian Structure: Destinies Altered

*Destinies altered through God's
Divine Structure*

Destinies Altered

Men and women dreaming of a better life founded our country upon mutual admiration and respect. They stood up for what they believed, and as a result, destinies were altered. Today we are beneficiaries of their dreams.

Our Founding Fathers mirrored the Trinitarian structure laid out in scripture consisting of the Father, Son, and Holy Spirit by creating three separate but unified branches of government: legislative, executive and judicial.

> For there are three that bear witness in heaven: the Father, the Word (Jesus/son), and the Holy Spirit; and these three are one.
> 1 John 5:7

> "They proposed a strong central government made up of three branches: legislative, executive, and judicial; each would be perpetually restrained by a sophisticated set of checks and balances." [9]

Our Father in heaven granted each one of us free will—the ability chose freely without fear of reprisal—without disrupting His divine order. The Trinitarian mirroring aspect of the *Declaration of Independence* is represented by honoring the free will of the people while preserving the country's core principles and beliefs.

> But one and the same Spirit works all these things, distributing to each one individually as He wills.
> 1 Corinthians 12:11

God didn't attempt to control, manipulate, or change who we were at the core when He created us and neither did our Founding Fathers. Quite the contrary, they established a biblical system whereby there would be checks and balances. They sought to safeguard the nation from one person or one group's ideals that could, if not held in check, influence and overturn the core principles and beliefs upon which the country was being founded. By establishing the three branches of government, balance was established and future growth secured.

We study history as a reminder of times past. It helps us understand and not forget the reason our forefathers came to this country in the first place and why they laid the foundation on such solid ground.

---

[9]*www.archives.gov/exhibits/charters/charters_of_freedom_6.html*

Mirroring God's instruction, our forefathers embraced the fact that people were going to disagree about how the country should be governed. They knew it was basic human nature for people to convince others that their way is the best.

Rather than be suspect of everyone with differing opinions, they set-up a government structure to deal with this inevitable reality of human behavior. They gave the people a say in the direction of the country by and through a system that allowed them to elect leaders. Once elected, those leaders were expected to represent the people's interests.

Today, we see elected officials influenced by lobbyists representing special interest groups. Oftentimes, these groups are motivated by selfish agendas that are not in the best interest of the people. These elected officials are not mirroring the example set by our Founding Fathers, and as a result, our nation is suffering.

Within each one of us there is a desire to be heard, a desire to change, a desire to make a difference, a desire to be great, and a desire to be accepted. Unfortunately, our intentions are not always pure and don't always have the interest of everyone in mind.

Over time, we have allowed our spiritual enemies, working through a political system, to rob us of the inalienable benefits we derive from living in one of the greatest countries on earth. Benefits endowed by our creator, God Himself. This should make us fighting mad and intent on mirroring the gospel of Jesus Christ.

The gospel is not a threat to our society, but the *lifeblood*, which will restore us, transform us, and ultimately lead to abundant life.

> The thief does not come except to steal, and to kill, and to destroy. I have come that they may have life, and that they may have it more abundantly.
> John 10:10

CLOSING
ETERNAL LIFE

> *And Jesus said to him, "Assuredly, I say to you, today you will be with Me in Paradise."*
> — Luke 23:43

In Matthew, we read the story how Jesus instructed a young man when he asked Jesus how to attain eternal life. Knowing the young man's heart, Jesus gave a response that demanded total devotion. The young man received an answer he was not expecting. He did not appear to be living a sinful life, but he wasn't prepared to give all for the greatest blessing imaginable. Today are we any different?

> Now behold, one came and said to Him, "Good Teacher, what good thing shall I do that I may have eternal life?" So He said to him, "Why do you call Me good? No one *is* good but One, *that is,* God. But if you want to enter into life, keep the commandments." He said to Him, "Which ones?" Jesus said, " *'You shall not murder,' 'You shall not commit adultery,' 'You shall not*

> steal,' 'You shall not bear false witness,' 'Honor your father and your mother,' and, 'You shall love your neighbor as yourself.' "The young man said to Him, "All these things I have kept from my youth. What do I still lack?" Jesus said to him, "If you want to be perfect, go, sell what you have and give to the poor, and you will have treasure in heaven; and come, follow Me." But when the young man heard that saying, he went away sorrowful, for he had great possessions.
>
> Matthew 19:16-22

Looking back over our shoulders at the past several years, we find society has experienced moral and ethical decay. This decay should be obvious. We need only to turn on the reality TV shows or visit the Internet. The decay is right there in plain view for our children and everyone to see. However, most people are content to ignore the effects or have become ignorant to the effects. Some Christians even seem to be complacent with regard to the erosion moral decay has caused. We have been content to embrace the lies that have broken down our foundational structures. Isn't it time to break free from those lies?

Jesus appeared to be challenging the young man to be perfect. Jesus knew no one could attain perfection or live up to God's standard. His counsel for the young man was to follow a path that would lead away from material possession to eternal treasure.

I started this writing citing an example of an athlete preparing for competition. Would the coach be wrong in demanding 100% devotion from the athlete? Would he or she be considered a great coach demanding anything less? Could the athlete rise to the highest level possible giving anything less than 100%? The Lord loves us and wants the best for us. He would not be a loving God if He asked anything less than 100% from us.

To mirror this point through the eyes of Christ, pretend Jesus is sitting right next to you. Ask Him these questions and try to perceive His response.

- Jesus, is it okay for us to have consensual sex outside of marriage?
- Jesus, is it all right for us to have a baby out of wedlock?
- Jesus, is it acceptable for us to abort a child?
- Jesus, is it okay if I tell a lie?
- Jesus, is it okay if I get drunk?
- Jesus, is it okay to murder a person?
- Jesus, is it okay to worship several gods?
- Jesus, is it okay to have idols?
- Jesus, is it okay to dishonor my Mother and Father?
- Jesus, is it okay to take your name in vain?
- Jesus, is it okay to covet my neighbor's possessions?
- Is it okay to practice any of these occasionally?

What do you think Jesus' answer would be? As a loving and perfect God, His only response would be to state emphatically, "No my child." His desire is that we would not commit sin. He does not control us, but instead, allows us to make choices that have resulting consequences.

Imagine your son or daughter asking, "Is it okay to entertain a little sin in my life?" Take a moment and then choose the response below that would best represent your counsel as a loving mother or father?

- Of course honey, you just live your life and don't worry about the consequences.
- You can choose to live any way you want, but you must accept the consequence that might result from your behavior.

By using the second response, we would not be challenging him or her to a life of perfection, but one of consequence. We would be mirroring the sound instruction of our Father in heaven.

Life is more about the process of being transformed by a loving Father, yet many Christians still embrace the lie that says, "If you were really a good person, you would never sin," or "If you were really a Christian, you wouldn't act that way." We are all guilty of some form of sin. Our response to a loving God is the true test of our spiritual character.

Like the young man in the passage from Matthew, none of us is perfect. If we ask God to search our hearts for some area of sin, He will reveal that sin to us, and it will be up to us to accept His rebuke and alter our behavior. Like our children, we must accept the responsibility for the consequences of our actions.

There is a bracelet many Christians are wearing that says "WWJD," which is an acronym meaning, "What Would Jesus Do?" Seems like an honest enough question. However, the only way you are going to see changes take place in your life and the life of others is to do what Jesus did. We must mirror His example.

Because we trust in Jesus Christ as our Lord and Savior, we are not void of sin, but we do, however, have power over sin. We have access to the same eternal treasure offered to the wealthy young man, a treasure reserved for God's children.

We need to stand strong and live according to biblical teaching. We must encourage one another through discipleship by mirroring Christ's behavior to others. We need to share our life experiences with others in order to provide hope. We need those relationships to assist us and hold us accountable to live lives free of a sinful nature.

Through His word, God has provided the answer to all of our questions, but it is up to us to sow His word into the hearts of His people. In so doing, we will be sowing biblical seed vital to the generational health of our families and our country.

There will always be the naysayers. They will attempt to thwart our efforts. They will accuse us of lecturing or poking our noses into other people's business. They would have us believe: our churches do not have a right to impose their doctrinal beliefs; teachers do not have a right to discipline our children; and law enforcement is made up of egotistical bullies attempting to control us.

As you speak biblical truth in the lives of others, you too might be accused of lecturing. Those making the accusation will most likely be trying to hide the truth, or they may be paranoid their past might be revealed.

If they are hiding a past life event, they falsely assume, if they can silence people with knowledge of their past, they can shield their shame. Well, that is a lie from the pit of hell because we all carry our pasts, and those pasts are there whether we like it or not. God's desire, however, is that we be set free from the sins of our past. Through biblical instruction, we learn the truth and uncover the hidden agenda of our fear; enslavement.

> To the Jews who had believed him, Jesus said, "If you hold to my teaching, you are really my disciples. Then you will know the truth, and the truth will set you free." They answered him, "We are Abraham's descendants and have never been slaves of anyone. How can you say that we shall be set free?" Jesus replied, "I tell you the truth, everyone who sins is a slave to sin. Now a slave has no permanent place in the family, but a son belongs to it forever.
>
> John 8:31-35

Our enemies want to block the impartation of eternal knowledge, which brings transformation into our lives. We need lecturers. Think about it, what do you get in college? You hear lectures. All of which are intended to educate you in certain subjects in order to prepare you for the degree you are seeking. If it were not for the lectures in life, we would not earn our degrees.

Speaking to the multitudes, Jesus imparted the Beatitudes to His followers in the Sermon on the Mount. Jesus was instructing them on the proper way to live their lives. He was sowing eternal seeds, seeds that continue to be sown every time someone reads or hears these words. How would Jesus be labeled today as a lecturer?

"Blessed are the poor in spirit, For theirs is the kingdom of heaven. Blessed are those who mourn, For they shall be comforted. Blessed are the meek, For they shall inherit the earth. Blessed are those who hunger and thirst for righteousness, For they shall be filled. Blessed are the merciful, For they shall obtain mercy. Blessed are the pure in heart, For they shall see God. Blessed are the peacemakers, For they shall be called sons of God. Blessed are those who are persecuted for righteousness' sake, For theirs is the kingdom of heaven. Blessed are you when they revile and persecute you, and say all kinds of evil against you falsely for My sake. Rejoice and be exceedingly glad, for great is your reward in heaven, for so they persecuted the prophets who were before you."

Matthew 5:3-12

Thus, we should all be proud to be one of the Lord's voices. There is something that happens in the spirit when we speak the word of God into people's lives. As we reflect Christ to one another through the spoken word, we reflect His goodness.

My natural father lectured me sowing eternal knowledge over the years. Unfortunately, he died at an early age. By the time I realized how important that knowledge was, he had passed away. Today, I would treasure an opportunity to thank him for taking the time to impart that knowledge. The fact that I cannot tell him makes me appreciate his wisdom even more. For that reason, I have sown wise seed into his grandchildren.

> "I am not so much concerned with who my grandfather was, but who his grandson has become."
>
> Abraham Lincoln

Moses and other great men of the bible originally passed down the history of their people orally from generation to generation. These were the teachings of God. We learn from scripture that people did not always want to hear what Moses had to say. The people were constantly grumbling.

> "Now this is the commandment, and these are the statutes and judgments which the LORD your God has commanded to teach you, that you may observe them in the land which you are crossing over to possess, that you may fear the LORD your God, to keep all His statutes and His commandments which I command you, you and your son and your grandson, all the days of your life, and that your days may be prolonged.
>
> Deuteronomy 6:1-2

> And the people spoke against God and against Moses: "Why have you brought us up out of Egypt to die in the wilderness? For there is no food and no water, and our soul loathes this worthless bread."
>
> Numbers 21:5

The people attempted to disqualify Moses because his message was not popular; it did not condone a sinful behavior. God had chosen Moses to be His messenger, to be His mirror if you will to deliver a message meant to transform them by the renewing of their minds. The message was meant to filter the lies and replace them with eternal truth.

Destructive forces are always attempting to silence and discredit the word of God. Those forces do not want God's children listening to reason.

> Hear, my children, the instruction of a father, And give attention to know understanding;
>
> Proverbs 4:1

Instruction from the natural Father should line up with God's word. Like Moses, we are to impart God's wisdom. For this reason, before we speak into someone's life, it is wise to preface our counsel by saying, "Discard those things which are of the flesh and let those things which are of the spirit penetrate deep into your soul." Impart the spiritual seeds of eternal truth, regardless of what they choose to believe.

> Then He spoke many things to them in parables, saying: "Behold, a sower went out to sow. And as he sowed, some seed fell by the wayside; and the birds came and devoured them. Some fell on stony places, where they did not have much earth; and they immediately sprang up because they had no depth of earth. But when the sun was up they were scorched, and because they had no root they withered away. And some fell among thorns, and the thorns sprang up and choked them. But others fell on good ground and yielded a crop: some a hundredfold, some sixty, some thirty. He who has ears to hear, let him hear!"
>
> Matthew 13:3-9

In the parable of the sower, Jesus was not so much concerned about the seed or the soil. He knew the seed was good, and he knew the soil of their hearts was moist and fertile ready to receive. Instead, He was warning them of a spiritual enemy. That enemy has a name, Satan. Satan is intent on snatching the good seed or through sin tainting the soil so that the seed would not take root.

When we buy into the enemy's sinful nature, we do immeasurable damage to the good soil that is contained within us. Everyone has fertile soil, but it is the sin and deception of sin that taints our soil. In the world in which we live, this parable is hard to understand. If we see that people are not embracing eternal truths or are ignorant in their understanding of them, we must pray for them to receive the seed of the word and for their ground to be fertile to receive the truth. Especially, we must pray for our children.

Through discipleship, we should rebuke the enemy on their behalf. We are called to be good stewards over the gardens God has put in our lives. We have a responsibility to assist His saints in the preparation of their soil. We must continue to sow good seed and pray for God to provide the nutrients for that seed.

> Who then is Paul, and who is Apollos, but ministers through whom you believed, as the Lord gave to each one? I planted, Apollos watered, but God gave the increase. So then neither he who plants is anything, nor he who waters, but God who gives the increase.
> 1 Corinthians 3:5-7

As we hold up a mirror to others based on our experiences, especially the painful experiences, hope is renewed. We are in essence instructing His children how to walk through troubled times toward His promised land. Through the mirroring process, lives are transformed and the power of the Holy Spirit realized. God brings the increase.

You will not always get a pat on the back. You will not always be recognized by the world. You will not always get to share in the success of others. However, God will see, and He will bestow upon you an eternal reward in heaven.

> In My Father's house are many mansions; if it were not so, I would have told you. I go to prepare a place for you.
>
> John 14:2

See you in heaven

ABOUT THE AUTHOR

I offer the following as a qualifier for writing *The Mirror Principle*.

I was born and raised in Dallas, Texas to a loving family. We attended church regularly up until my 6th grade year. I didn't know it at the time, but my father was on the board of stewards at our church. One Saturday he was called to a special meeting where he learned that the other elders were plotting to fire the minister. Caught off guard, he rose from his seat and exited the room determined not to be a part of what he deemed to be an underhanded ploy by a few to control the altar. He resigned his leadership role and we began attending less. You could say that we became holiday Christians. We attended church faithfully on all the major holidays, but Sundays were spent on the golf course.

Our exit from the church happened at a time in my life when I needed the church's influence more than ever, especially as I entered adolescence. Not having a solid spiritual influence gave way for me to travel down a destructive path. In time alcohol and drugs became my constant companions.

When I was in eighth grade my father was in the beginning stages of lung cancer. Of course, no one in the family knew about his failing health. He finally let us in on the diagnoses when he had to have a lung removed. Fear engulfed my mother's heart and through my high school years she and my father spent every day together. My older brothers were already out of the house and my parents thought I was pretty well adjusted and so they began to travel. Looking back, I understand they realized their time together was limited, but not having the necessary supervision allowed me freedom to explore areas of life that were not healthy. Fortunately, I was a pretty good student and graduated at the top of my class. Otherwise, I would never have been able to attend Texas A&M University.

Upon entering college, I toned down a good portion of my negative life style, but those who knew me back then would beg to differ. My saving grace was joining a fraternity. Virtue, diligence and brotherly love were the tenets that the fraternity was based upon and provided a positive influence. This helped me to finish strong and graduate in four years. Dad died the year after I graduated; I was twenty three at the time.

I accepted my first job in Dallas from a broker operating out of the Dallas Apparel Mart. He hired me to represent his lines in the states of Louisiana, Mississippi and Arkansas. Having New Orleans as one of my strongest markets, I embarked on a wild adventure. My boss was a good business man, but unfortunately he was also an alcoholic. If

About The Author

I could keep him sober through lunch we would have a productive day. One night after rolling him to the showroom on one of our clothing racks, a common occurrence, I made the decision that a change was in order. The time with him had been an exciting experience, but not conducive to a long-term positive outcome. I resigned and began a career in restaurant management where I quickly rose through the ranks and became a general manager with a national chain.

My lifestyle had not changed much, but slowly I began adjusting my behavior patterns for the better. It was about that time I met a girl while managing a restaurant in Phoenix who would later be my wife and the mother of my children. She was a student and I was just beginning my food-service career. We continued dating after I was transferred to Florida. Looking back, I made the biggest mistake of my life: I let her drop out of school and come live with me. Soon I was promoted and we moved to Ohio where we continued to live out of wedlock. I remember asking myself, "If you plan on spending the rest of your life with her then ask her to marry you." I did and we moved to Dallas and were married in an Episcopal Church.

The first year we were married she was lured into an adulteress relationship with a married man who had two children. I found a poem he had written and after putting the pieces together became aware of the affair. It was the most devastating time in my life up to that point. After confronting her we spent a lot of time talking, but I never got an answer as to why she had the affair. I contentedly justified her behavior by thinking that I had lived a pretty wild life and that being younger she just needed to sow her wild oats. We agreed to counseling and I made the decision to forgive her. The Priest chosen for the task was quiet and intimidating. So instead of continuing the sessions we just started attending church on regular basis. We were just hiding in church putting up a pretty front that said, "We are happy." We avoided digging into either of our pasts to uncover the reasons for her infidelity. A condition of our continuing marriage was that she would resign her position and find a new job. This decision put her on a path to fulfill her inner passion.

For a while everything seemed to settle down and appeared to be falling into place. My career started taking off and she loved her new design position with a popular Dallas developer. Unfortunately, during this period we learned that one of my brothers was an alcoholic and I was tasked to check him into treatment. My current employer wouldn't give me time off to attend a family weekend so I had to use vacation time. This created resentment on my part that would later be damaging to my career. Soon after I was asked to vacate my position so I started a manufacturing company. It wasn't long until she was pregnant with our second son. The next year went by smoothly and we appeared to our friends as the model couple. My business was booming and then tragedy hit again, the developer she was working for started laying off staff. Her positon was vulnerable so I suggested she resign and we would start a design firm. Clients in the building gave her a start and she never looked back. Over the years the firm became a sustaining business in her life.

About The Author

Then I began to notice a change in her behavior which reminded me of a pattern played out when she had her previous affair. She made plans to take our kids to visit her mother and sister in Florida, but the details of the trip were sketchy. I had been in training for five months to participate on a weekend Kairos ministry at a maximum security prison in central Texas. Her timing seemed curious since I was not going to be able to join them, but I didn't object. When I returned from the ministry weekend I tried to reach her by phone but her mother and sister gave conflicting accounts of her whereabouts. I had a sense that something was wrong. So I called my Brother and the two of us uncovered that a man she worked with had traveled to Florida to be with her. We learned his flight information from the airline and discovered the hotel where he was staying. We even went to the airport and saw him disembark from the plane so we were sure that he had made the trip. Deceptively she had left the kids with her mother and sister and joined him at a local hotel.

When she returned home I confronted her in front of a Priest from our church and she admitted to having the affair. This time she was determined to marry the individual. I also learned that she had not ended the first affair right away. Needless to say, my whole world was turned upside down. I pleaded for the two of us to remain married by stating, "We have two great sons, all we have to do is be honest and put the past behind us." She was not in agreement and our worlds were forever changed through divorce. The enemy had finally succeeded in dividing our young family.

Having been awarded custody of our children I spent the next six years as a single father struggling to keep a business together and raise my boys. They were two and four at the time. As is usually the case, her lover had some serious personal issues and the two of them called it quits. She was able to purchase a home out of their separation, but her life was not in a good place. She began attending a non-denominational church where she had a born-again experience. Being suspect I kept my distance and attempted to set a good example for our children. She continued the process of putting her life back together.

Life seemed good, the boys were in martial arts and playing sports and my business was doing well. I was very involved in ministry at the church and was growing spiritually, but I didn't know anything about Lordship. Then some friends at church introduced me to a single mother and I fell heads over heals for her. I didn't think I was capable of the feelings I was having and before long we were joined physically. I had confused lust for love and used the excuse that we were consenting adults to condone sexual intercourse. I was hooked and before long I asked her to marry me. After the wedding, I found a new home and she and her young daughter came to live with us. It wasn't long before the boy's mother became jealous of the amount of time she was spending with our sons. She started making false accusations about my new wife to the parents where our boys attended school. Then she and her new boyfriend filed a law suit seeking custody of the boys.

This was a confusing time for my sons. My youngest didn't really understand what was going on, but my oldest knew that their life had changed forever. I remember shooting baskets with him when out of the blue he said, "I'm not going to any court." We sat down and I asked what he had meant. He related that his mother and her boyfriend had approached him about making a choice before a judge about where he wanted to live. I looked him in the eye and asked what he wanted. He said, "I just want to spend time with the two of you when I want." I told him that I would do everything in my power to make that happen and to keep him from going in front of a judge.

I sought mediation and the resulting agreement cost me dearly and in the long run it wasn't easy, but I can always look to that day and know that I kept my promise to my son. With everything taking place it was all I could do to keep my business a float and maintain some semblance of a balanced home life. In the midst of all the turmoil my new wife decided to have an affair. Before long an identical scenario played out and I experienced another painful divorce. The way I found out was similar to the first time I was faced with an adulteress situation. My life and my children's lives were upended once more and I felt like a failure.

Fortunately, members of my church that were close friends encouraged me to stay active. I entered a program with my sons called "Guardian Angels" and through that experience received deep inner healing. I learned a painful lesson that by attempting to use sexual intimacy to fill my broken heart I was doomed to the same outcome in life. My second marriage had been a rebound marriage and I had not been mentally or spiritually ready to embark on another marriage. Throughout this time, The Lord had a plan for my life and His desire was to have a personal relationship with me. He wanted me to allow Him into my heart so He could bring eternal healing. He had allowed me to go around the same mountain again to bring me to a point of surrender. When I detoured off His intended path and pursued a sexual relationship outside of marriage I found myself caught in swirl of insanity—doing the same thing, but expecting a different result.

Their mother had changed non-denominational churches and our boys were going to be in a children's play. They asked if I would attend and, not one to deny my children, I consented. Upon walking in, a person who later would become a good friend was playing the electric guitar. I remember saying to myself, "Where have you been?" I thoroughly enjoyed the service; in fact, I asked my boys if they wanted to return the following weekend. I was drawn to the different style of worship. The next Sunday at the conclusion of the service, the Pastor began a routine altar call. He began by asking if anyone wanted to put their trust in Christ to come up front. But suddenly he paused and said, "Some of you have already done that, maybe you need to come down front and reaffirm Him as The Lord of your life." At the same time, I was thinking, "I've already done that." I don't remember leaving my seat, but I went down and he prayed over me. From that day forward the bible came alive like never before. Soon after I had a supernatural baptism and I dedicated my life to Christ in a fresh new way. God has a sense of humor, I found Lordship in the church of a women who wasn't on my most wanted list.

About the Author

I have never shared my story in an open format for fear of hurting my sons. However, over the years I have come to realize that the more we suppress the truth the more others speculate about our past. We all need permission to open up and share our pain. Not with the intention of hurting others, but to allow The Lord to enter those painful areas and heal our hearts. When we are vulnerable, other people in our sphere of influence learn that they too can share their pain. Guided by painful testimonies some learn to alter their lives in a positive way and avoid the same mistakes that others have experienced. The Bible tells us that the truth will set us free. So I repeat, we don't share our stories to hurt anyone—we share openly so others can be healed.

The Lord taught me an incredible lesson through this painful time. A lesson that at first was hard to embrace—I was the one responsible for both of my wife's infidelity. I wasn't directly responsible, but from a spiritual perspective, I was totally responsible. Had I originally treated them with respect and conducted myself in a Godly manner their life course might have been altered. I might have been the one true friend they could have turned to in order to work through the pain of their past. All our lives might have turned out differently.

As a result of these painful experiences, I have been able to provide counsel for many young people. One thing I always say to them if they are in relationship is, "If you plan to spend the rest of your life with this person then get to know their heart." God knows our hearts intimately and when we invite him into our lives he will not only reveal other people's hearts to us He will reveal what is in our own heart.

During this time I entered the ministry becoming ordained through Victory New Testament Fellowship International and began traveling on the mission field. I spent the majority of my time in Cuba where I learned firsthand the devastation that communism inflicts. My travels prompted me to write a book, Freedom from S.I.N., where the title is an acronym for Satan's Intended Notion. In the book, I reveal a second acronym, Societal in Nature. Given the fact that we all have sin residing in our heart I learned we are the ones carrying out Satan's evil. Like I experienced in my own life, moral and ethical decay is rampant in the world we live in. Unfortunately, the same decay is present in many of our churches. It is time we opened our hearts to see the world from a spiritual perspective. This is accomplished by identifying Satan's antics and drawing the parallel being carried out by people in the various societies on earth. Temptations, deceptions and accusations are being falsely levied at well-meaning people. Satan is the tempter, the deceiver and the accuser. We have become ignorant how he manipulates the sin in men and women's hearts. In my story the fault was not that of my former spouses or mine, the fault was the sin residing in each of our hearts.

> So the great dragon was cast out, that serpent of old, called the Devil and Satan, who deceives the whole world; he was cast to the earth, and his angels were cast out with him. Then I heard a loud voice saying in heaven, "Now salvation, and strength, and the kingdom of our God, and the power of His Christ have come, for the accuser of our brethren, who ac-

About The Author

cused them before our God day and night, has been cast down.

Revelation 12:9-10 (NKJV)

Using my painful experiences and my writing The Lord has allowed me to mentor incarcerated youth at a local detention center. Only 10% of the young men I meet with have positive relationships with their natural fathers. It breaks my heart to hear their stories, but I am blessed to have a wonderful stage where God shows up to alter their destinies. This ministry has had the most profound effect on my life and I pray the Lord will allow me to continue as long as I can walk and talk.

About twelve years ago I wrote a note to The Lord telling him what I desired in a mate. Time was of no concern and sixteen years had passed since my divorce. Attending a memorial service for a friend's mother I met an incredible woman of God that is full of love and joy. Two years later we were married and now we are enjoying the spiritual love that God had intended for us all along.

Our Lord is a God of many chances so don't lose heart, grab hold of Him and He will never let you go.

OTHER BOOKS
BY LAWRENCE P. LUBY

FREEDOM FROM S.I.N.
SATAN'S INTENDED NOTION / SOCIETAL IN NATURE

S.I.N., satan's intended notion for our lives, has a firm grip on our society, families, churches, and on us. This book exposes the enemy's efforts to divide us and offers hope for overcoming the effects of sin.

Naturally, we pull away from conflict, but freedom comes when we do the opposite of our inclinations. By moving beyond quick fixes and embracing true deliverance, keys to the kingdom are found. God's system of free will leads us to experience life as He intended it to be as practice rounds of spiritual preparation. As we learn to submit to the Triune God, we gain the covering God desires to provide until we reach our eternal destination.

FREEDOM FROM S.I.N.
CORRESPONDING NINE-WEEK STUDY GUIDE

Cairo Unzipped
Written for Mona Fuad
Based on a True Story

It's the 1940's, and the desert sun is setting on Cairo. Layla, a beautiful young girl forced into prostitution at age 12 by her mother, dreams of freedom in Europe. However, with no money and few options, Layla dives into a treacherous world few ever escape. Little does she know that she will not only survive the life of a call girl, but also rise to become mistress to King Farouk, the most powerful man in Egypt.

Cairo Unzipped tracks Layla's meteoric rise during the most fascinating period in Egyptian history. Due to the turmoil in Europe, Egypt became a melting pot of Europeans from nations being put to the fire by the Nazis. European influences flourished, modernizing the country but causing dangerous cultural friction. The handsome, young King Farouk fit the times of Egypt perfectly, just as Gandhi fit the times of India, but the clock was ticking on this golden age in Egypt, and revolution was afoot. After being overthrown and exiled in 1952, King Farouk dropped dead in Italy at age 45, an event shrouded in mystery. This story unveils that mystery and takes you on a journey of historical proportions.

COMING SOON

PLUGGED INTO GOD
GOD'S POWER STRIP: THE ULTIMATE POWER SOURCE

We all know what a power strip is, that wonderful device which allows us to plug in a variety of items. The power strip serves two unique purposes: it—gives us access to one source of power, and it protects us from electrical surges.

These surges can cause damage to our computers and other precious electronics. We work with sources of power every day, and the source of that power is usually hidden from our view. For example, we turn on our coffee in the morning and can see the cord plugged into the wall, but we do not see the current flow to the pot. We flip a switch on the wall, and the lights come on, but we do not see the source of the power. Many items we use are wireless, but without power, they will not operate. At some level, they too are plugged into a power source, one we do not see but cannot deny.

For years, we have been infatuated with stories about the supernatural. These stories appeal to us because somewhere deep inside our being, we long to tap into a power source. We desire a power source that can provide an unlimited source of energy.

To purchase these and other books please
visit the publisher's website:

www.hispublish.com